MIDDLE SCHOOL BULLETIN BOARDS

written and illustrated by Judy Hierstein

cover design by Judy Hierstein

Publisher
Instructional Fair • TS Denison
Grand Rapids, Michigan 49544

ISBN: 1-56822-548-2
Middle School Bulletin Boards
Copyright © 1997 by Instructional Fair • TS Denison
2400 Turner Avenue NW
Grand Rapids, Michigan 49544

TABLE OF CONTENTS

TO THE TEACHER

Most teachers, even those who are artistic, dread bulletin boards. They seem to take so much time and effort in an already demanding schedule. Yet bright, eye-catching displays do much to improve the atmosphere in the classroom, providing an atmosphere necessary for learning to take place. Bulletin boards that visually reinforce the subject material are doubly beneficial. If you could only get someone else to design and install them . . . .

. . . That's where this book comes in. It is filled with great ideas for bulletin boards, simple and inexpensive, that students can do themselves. Suggestions for materials and color schemes are included and layout and specially designed title lettering is illustrated, which can be enlarged and utilized or replaced with a student's own creative ideas.

Each board is a learning experience for students as they are often asked to research a topic in the preparation of the display. The topics cover concepts taught in the middle school curriculum, as well as seasonal celebrations, current events issues, "healthy self" issues dealing with the social and emotional health in today's stressful society, and some interesting ideas from around the world. The creation of the bulletin board, including research, can be used as a student or group unit project, and the board itself serves as the visual aid as the information is shared with the class. Because the board stays up, the material can be reviewed by students at their leisure so that more of the information is retained . . .

. . . And your classroom looks great!

How to Best Use This Resource

Teachers have long known that students learn best in a variety of ways. No two students are alike. The ideas for bulletin boards presented in this resource book are designed to enhance the learning taking place in several ways—with the hands-on approach necessary in the creation and arrangement of the boards and the visual reinforcement that the finished board provides in your classroom. In addition, research skills are reinforced in gathering information to complete the boards.

Once an idea for a board has been chosen, you may choose to follow the recommendations, or you may want to select those pieces which will best benefit your class. Each idea is illustrated with a title and art work which may be reproduced by enlargement (see below), copied freehand by an artistic student, or discarded entirely for a better idea that a student may have!

To enlarge art work in this book:
Use your copy machine to make a copy of the idea to be enlarged onto a sheet of acetate, and place it in an overhead projector to project the image onto the board or a large sheet of paper with the same measurements as the board. Trace the image in pencil first, making certain that this process is completed in one session to avoid the complication of realigning the projector.

Place the page from the book to be enlarged in an opaque projector and repeat the above process.

If you do not have access to the equipment necessary for the methods suggested above, the grid system may be used. Divide a copy of the page into squares, and divide the paper covered board into an equal number of larger squares in roughly the same proportion. Carefully copy each small square onto its corresponding larger square.

If only the letters of the title are to be reproduced, simply set your copy machine to the highest enlargement setting and then enlarge the enlargement until the desired size is achieved. Use these copies as patterns to cut your letters.

SOURCES OF FREE AND NEARLY FREE MATERIALS

Resources are always in short supply, but that does not mean you cannot have a creative and attractive room. When designing these bulletin boards, keep in mind that it is the unusual materials that are often the most interesting and the least expensive. Everything that goes on a board need not be flat. Three-dimensional objects, so long as they are not too heavy, can be added for greater textural contract. Discarded paintings can be cut up for decorative lettering. Gift wrapping and wallpaper samples also become interesting composition materials. Actual objects, such as old clothing, can be trimmed and pinned to the board to add texture, interest, and realism.

Some communities have WasteSHARE®, affiliated with the public schools, which collects (safe) materials that businesses would ordinarily throw away and makes them available to teachers free of charge. It saves the teachers a lot of time because they can go to one place instead of contacting community businesses individually.

Hospitals are often willing to give old sterile sheets that can no longer be repaired, and they make great background drapes for boards, especially when tie-dyed or painted.

Newspapers, especially comic strips, make interesting and colorful backgrounds appropriate for some displays.

If you have a printing company in your area, they often have offsize paper scraps left over from a run that they will donate to schools.

Colorful envelopes from greeting cards are discarded when the card becomes out of date. Ask at drug stores if you might ask the card vendor for some.

Your own students are a good source of discarded materials. Ask them to bring in materials to be used on bulletin boards.

HEY! HI!

Even though by now middle school students have done all this before—many times—there is still a certain amount of excited anticipation when it is once again time for school to start in the fall. Welcome them back this year with this quick and easy idea.

You will need:
>   White background paper
>   Black construction paper (or any black paper)
>   Markers

DIRECTIONS:

Cover the bulletin board or display area with white paper, such as newsprint, and cut out letters to spell the title "Sign In, Please" or "Hey! Hi!" Attach the letters to the center of the board and have each student sign the blank board with a colorful marker as they enter the room. By the end of the day you will have a ready-made bulletin board. Leave it up for at least a week and once everyone has had a chance to sign it, you may ask students to fill in any of the empty spaces with messages to their friends or their favorite song from the summer or anything they would like to write publicly (so long as it is acceptable).

ARE YOU READY?

All teachers are provided with a school calendar, complete with holidays and breaks, in-service days, and special school events that will take place over the next nine months. When students come back to school in the fall, map out the year for them on one of the bulletin boards. This will help them to order their world in terms of project deadlines, topics studied, and long-awaited holidays. It may even help you, too.

You will need:
> White background paper
> Construction or other colored paper in at least four colors
> Thick and thin markers
> Stickers (1" circles)

DIRECTIONS:

Cover the board with solid white paper. Allowing for about a 6" margin all around, divide the remaining area into 21 equal spaces across and 15 equal spaces down. Use a black marker to draw these grid lines onto the white paper on the bulletin board. Darken the seventh and fourteenth vertical lines and the outside edges, and write the title "Are You Ready?" in script across the top margin. Continue with a scribbly black line around the grid, as shown. Cut several colors of construction paper rectangles on the paper cutter slightly smaller than the measurements of the individual rectangles of the grid you have drawn. Have students use the school calendar for the year to staple these onto the grid, using a different color to represent each month, and marking the date on each one. When the basic calendar is finished, cut additional rectangles from a bright color which has not already appeared to represent vacation days and staple them over the appropriate days. Have students customize this calendar by adding confetti-like dots of color around the border with markers, designing special rectangles for their birthdays, holidays, and breaks, or copy and color the samples given on the following pages. Keep track of the time which has elapsed by adding a 1" circle sticker to each day that passes.

This will be a bright and cheerful addition to your room, but it will also be useful. When a long-term project is assigned, it can be marked on the calendar. Deadlines cannot sneak up on students or you. The calendar can also be used to note significant events that occur during the year, either within the school or around the world.

As long as the additions and customized rectangles made for the bulletin board are stapled in place and not glued to the grid, it can be saved and reused from year to year. Simply remove the staples from the colored rectangles, discarding and replacing only those that have become out of date and stapling them in their new correct spot each year.

Are You Ready?

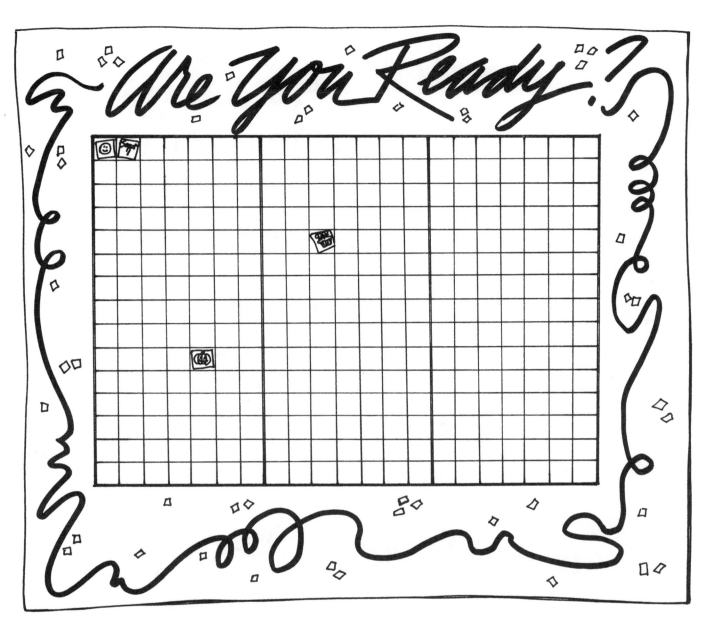

WINTER BREAK

this day is OVER!

6

MASCOT MANIA

Every school has its own special mascot. Make the most of yours and boost school spirit with this bulletin board idea that can last through the year.

You will need:

Paper to cover the board in one of your school colors
White paper to draw a large version of the school mascot
Poster-size paper of another school color
Paints or markers
Items of discarded clothing

DIRECTIONS:

Cover the bulletin board with paper (or cloth, felt, etc.) in one of your school colors. Reproduce your school mascot about student-size on a large piece of white paper, in a pose similar to the mascot illustrated, or draw a cartoon version of your mascot. Paint this figure with tempera and add details appropriate to the nature of the creature, such as fake fur, feathers, felt, etc. Cut the figure out and add it to the bulletin board on the left-hand side. Cut out letters to spell the title "I'm All Yours" from paper in your other school colors and place them across the top of the board. Place smaller letters cut from black or white, whichever contrasts better on top of the larger letters. Cut a poster-sized rectangle in the same color as the letters and place it to the right of the mascot.

This basic bulletin board can stay up all year. In the fall, staple a school folder to the mascot's hand and staple an actual T-shirt over the body so that it appears as though the mascot is wearing it. Make a sign on a sheet of white paper cut slightly smaller than the poster that welcomes students and staple it onto the poster on the bulletin board. Give the mascot a football jersey for the first big game and replace the notebook with a full-size drawing of a football; add a mask at Halloween and advertise the dance in the poster area. Have it don a Santa hat at Christmas; staple on an actual knit sweater and scarf when the weather gets cold. Dress it as the lead character in the school play, and give it shades and tropical shirt when summer rolls around again. Ask school clubs to take a turn dressing the mascot and advertising their activities. Put an apron around its waist and a message about a bake sale in the poster area or a sudsy dripping sponge in its hand for a car wash—whatever!

FALLING FOR FALL

This generic fall bulletin board works well as a background for fall activities across the curriculum.

You will need:

        Black or bright blue background paper
        Brown paper bags
        Autumn leaves collected along the roadside

DIRECTIONS:

Cover the bulletin board with black or bright blue paper; then reproduce the letters "Fall" onto brown paper bags that have been cut open so that they lay flat and can be pieced together. Attach the paper bag letters onto the center of the background; then staple an array of colorful autumn leaves onto the brown letters, leaving ample room around the title to fill with a project of your choice, such as one of the following:

The meaning of the word—have each student write a short sentence or phrase including the word "fall" in one of its various meanings. Examples: Because of the force of gravity, an object will fall to the ground. Don't fall for that old trick. "The Fall of the House of Usher." *Legends of the Fall.* Foliage falls in fall. To fall in love is a curious phenomenon. I hope our plans don't fall through. Fall back and faint. Here's a joke that won't fall flat.

Activities for fall—Post dates of football games and other important school and community events of interest to students.

Have students write short humorous or serious poems about "falling."

Study the seasons—fall in particular. Assign each student one fall change to write about. Why do the days get shorter? Why do the leaves change color? Why do they fall from the trees? Why is it springtime in Australia? What is the autumnal equinox?

Use the board as a welcome and reminder of school rules and students' responsibilities. Add tips for success, such as where, when, and how to study.

For newcomers to the school in your homeroom, attach school photos of teachers and the subjects they teach along with their room numbers. You may even wish to include a small labeled map of the school.

GOOD LUCK THIS YEAR

Of course, a successful school involves a great deal of effort, work, study, enthusiasm, and a positive attitude. But it never hurts to add a little luck to the mix with this well-wishing bulletin board idea.

You will need:
>   Solid, dark background paper (the darkest of your own school colors, perhaps)
>   Gold or silver foil paper or aluminum foil
>   Assorted "charming" found objects

DIRECTIONS:

Begin this bulletin board project by wishing all students good luck in the upcoming school year and then discuss exactly what students think it means to wish someone good luck. People used to be much more superstitious than they are today. The ancient Egyptians as well as the Incas revered the cat for its luck. But the cat was thought to be unlucky in the Middle Ages even though it helped control rats that carried the Plague.

While science has explained many things we once believed were magical, most cultures still retain some practices to ensure good luck. In our culture, many people carry a rabbit's foot, coin or medal, or wear a lucky locket. Some hang horseshoes by their doors (right-side-up so the luck won't fall out) or cross their fingers or take great care not to walk under a ladder or to break a mirror. Some toss salt over their shoulders, and many people still feel uneasy when a black cat crosses their path! Ask students whether they practice any rituals to keep them lucky.

Have each student bring one small item or a drawing of an item that could be used as a good luck charm. They then can research "luck" to discover a surefire lucky practice and write up their findings on a small piece of paper. Mount each paper on a slightly larger piece of foil. Cover the bulletin board with a solid color of background paper; then, using foil, cut out letters to spell the title "Good Luck." (Gold and silver always have a "lucky" feel about them.) Attach the letters to the board. Around them, add the items and notes produced by students. Staple additional scraps of foil and add some foil star stickers.

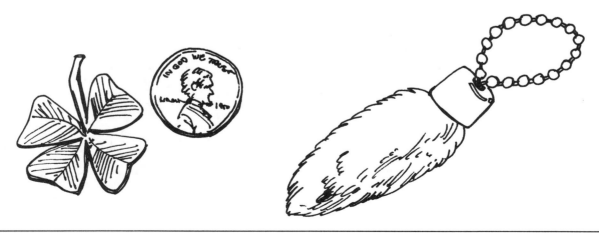

13

CELEBRATE THE SEASON

Whether your students observe Christmas, Hanukkah, Kwanzaa, or another holiday, bring the spirit of the season to your school with this bulletin board idea.

You will need:

Dark blue or black paper to cover the bulletin board
White paper for title and large snowflakes
Crystal glitter (optional)

DIRECTIONS:

As December draws near, the excitement of the holidays fills the air. Students are looking forward to some free time during the break and so are teachers. Take advantage of this festive spirit to look more closely into what, why, and how people celebrate. Begin by discussing the Christian holiday of Christmas and the origin of this holiday. Most American children are familiar with this holiday whether they are accustomed to celebrating it or not. Discuss Santa Claus (St. Nicolas) and his beginnings and some of the family holiday traditions students in the class may observe. If you have students who celebrate Hanukkah, conduct a similar discussion about that religious celebration. Kwanzaa is another celebration some of your students may observe. Begun in 1966, it is an African-American celebration of the unity of the family based on traditional African harvest festivals. The word is Swahili meaning "First Fruit." Observation of this fairly new tradition takes place from December 26 through January 1, with a huge feast called *Karamu* held on the seventh and final day. The Hindus celebrate a harvest festival called *Diwali*; the Chinese have a Moon Festival in the fall and the Chinese New Year is celebrated sometime in January or February.

Cover the bulletin board with solid dark blue or black paper and staple small white circles to represent snow. Cut letters to spell the title "Happy Holidays" or "Celebrate the Season" from white paper and attach these to the center of the board. Fold a few 12" x 12" sheets of thin white paper in half three times and cut them to make large snowflakes as shown. Crystal glitter may be added to the snow dots and the letters. Working individually or in small groups, have the class explore the various holidays observed around the world during this season of the year. They should present their findings with colorful photos, drawings, and short paragraphs that can be placed on the bulletin board, each overlapping a large snowflake, once students have explained them to the class.

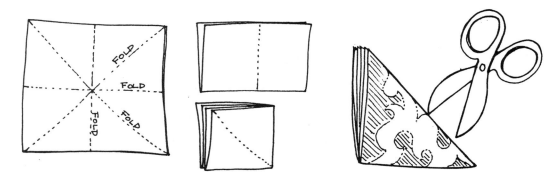

ADVENTURE AWAITS

As summer draws near and thoughts turn to the long, lazy vacation stretching out endlessly, allow students to dream a little dream with this bulletin board idea.

You will need:
>Solid color paper to cover the bulletin board
>World map (or paper on which to reproduce one)
>Black markers
>Colored chalk or pencils
>Colored string or yarn
>Travel brochures

DIRECTIONS:

Ask students if they and their families have any travel plans for summer vacation. Are they going on a trip? Where? Where would they like to go if they could? Discuss possible dream vacations: Disney World, an Alaskan cruise, white water rafting on the Colorado River, mountain climbing in the Himalayas, exploring China, India, or the ancient ruins at Machu Picchu. Have students work individually or in small groups and choose a dream vacation they have always wanted to take. They then research the spot to find the route, the cost, the mode of transportation, the sights to see, and the essentials to take along.

The research may either begin in the library or may begin with a trip to a local travel agent. Each student or group will prepare a short report, complete with brochures and illustrations and a brief outline to tell the class of their plans. Cover the board with any solid color and attach a map of the world in the center of the board. If a map is unavailable, have students reproduce the map shown in this unit using an opaque projector or an overhead projector and an acetate copy. Trace the map with a black marker and use chalk or colored pencils to color it in. Reproduce the title "Adventure Awaits" or use a similar style of letters to write "Bon Voyage" or "Off We Go!" Attach the travel plans to the bulletin board around the map and tack one end of a string or yarn to the vacation spot and the other end to the report.

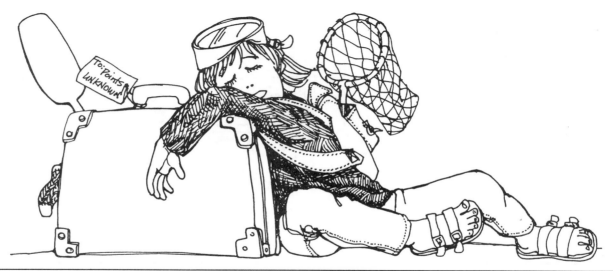

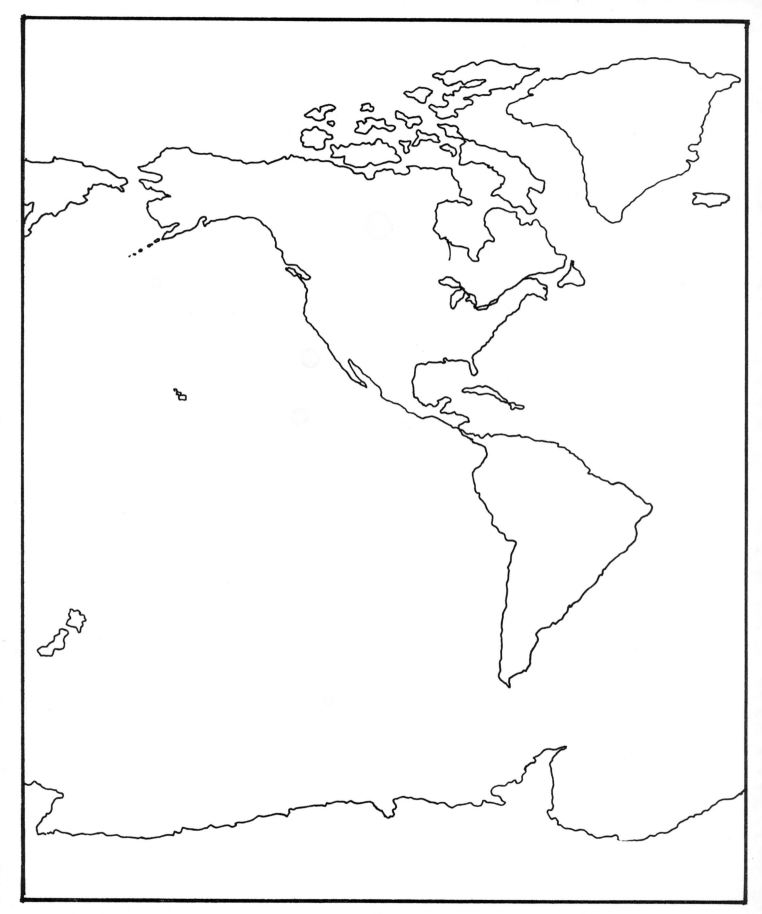

THE END

Just as you opened the year with a bulletin board that welcomed the students with their own comments, "Sign In, Please," bring closure to the year with a "sign out" board.

You will need:

      White paper to cover the bulletin board
      Markers of all colors
      Mementos of the year
      Bright construction paper or recycled gift wrap
      Black construction paper

DIRECTIONS:

By the end of the year, most students (and teachers) begin counting the days. When the number gets short, spend a few minutes reminiscing about the year. Have students made new friends or changed their way of looking at issues? Do they feel they have grown as human beings? Is there some friend or teacher they feel has made a special effort to help them out? Did some memorable event happen which they will never forget?

Cover the bulletin board with white paper and cut out the letters to spell the words "The End" from assorted colors of bright construction paper or recycled gift wrap. Cut an identical set from black construction paper and place these letters behind the colored letters so that the letters appear to have a shadow. Attach the letters across the top of the bulletin board and leave the markers lying nearby. Allow students to take turns signing their names and writing their good-byes and special messages about the past year. If you or your students have saved ticket stubs or programs or plastic strips off pom pons, these may be added as well.

22

COMMUNICATION

Many animals, from honeybees to chimpanzees, have evolved methods of communication. Humans have turned this survival skill into a fine art with a myriad of ways of exchanging messages. This bulletin board idea is a great starter for any English or foreign language class.

You will need:
> Bright solid colored paper to cover the bulletin board
> Markers
> Construction paper
> White paper

DIRECTIONS:

Ask students to brainstorm about the ways in which humans communicate. Remember, we may use any or all of the five senses and that the art of communication has evolved over many years, with inventions and machines. Here are some possibilities:

> Cave Paintings
> Smoke Signals
> Alphabets
> Morse Code
> Semaphore
> Secret Codes
> Mental Telepathy
> Facial Expressions
> Body Language
> Sign Language
> Shorthand
> Letters and Post Cards
> Radio
> Television
> Computers, E-mail, Internet

Measure a bulletin board that has been covered with a solid bright color and divide it into roughly 10- or 12-inch squares. Across one row of squares, attach 13 white squares (4" x 4") with the letters "C-O-M-M-U-N-I-C-A-T-I-O-N" written on them in block style with black markers. Copy the symbols of the five senses with black markers onto five different colors of construction paper cut in 8" squares and place these below the letters. Have students work individually or in small groups to explore one of the methods of communication that has been discussed in greater depth. They then can prepare a visual presentation of their findings in a square format that measures one-half inch smaller than the squares into which the bulletin board has been divided, as illustrated. Depending on which communication method has been chosen, the display may be in the form of a short paragraph, an illustration, or preferably both. When the reports are ready, have each student or group present their work to the class as they add it to the board.

PALINDROMES

William Irvine describes the palindrome as, "Wordplay for the ambidextrous mind. . . ." Sharpen the dexterity of students' minds with this entertaining activity and colorful bulletin board.

You will need:
      Large white paper cut to the size of the bulletin board
      Tempera paints
      White paper in two- to three-inch-wide strips
      Markers

DIRECTIONS:

Palindromes are simple sentences and phrases which read exactly the same backwards as forwards. But they are not nearly so simple to think of as you may think! Introduce the concept of palindromes to the class and give them several examples such as these:

MADAM, I'M ADAM
SENILE FELINES
O, GNATS TANGO
IF I HAD A HI-FI
TEPEE PET
STOLE COYOTE TOY, OCELOTS?
A RAGA IN NIAGARA
EEL GLEE
POTS, NONSTOP
SPIT Q-TIPS
TACO CAT
NEIL, AN ALIEN
WORM ROW
DESSERTS, I STRESSED
POOR DAN IS IN A DROOP
SEPARATE TAR APES
SOME MEN INTERPRET NINE MEMOS
PETS NIP INSTEP

And, of course, the ever popular "ABLE WAS I ERE I SAW ELBA," purportedly uttered by Napoleon when he was exiled, provides an interesting example. Present these and other palindromes you may know to your students. Then, give them a few days to come up with palindromes of their own and use markers to write them in capital letters onto strips of white paper. Cut large block letters to spell the title "WOW" from black construction paper. Cut a piece of white paper to fit the board or fit several smaller sheets together and tape along the seams on the back. Fold the sheet in half vertically; then open it up and lay it on a newspaper-covered surface. Working quickly, apply thick squiggles and swirls of tempera paint onto one side of the white paper. Carefully refold it and press the two sides together firmly, smoothing with hands to spread the paint between the layers. Open the paper up gently to reveal a design that, like a palindrome, is the same on both sides. If students are disappointed with the design, they can add more paint where needed and refold the paper until they attain desired results. Attach it to the bulletin board when it has thoroughly dried, and add the title letters and the students' palindromes all centered on the painted background, one below another.

BRILLIANT DEDUCTIONS

We are all familiar with Sir Arthur Conan Doyle's famous sleuth, Sherlock Holmes. His name is synonymous with the clever art of deduction. Increase the deductive powers of your class with this bulletin board idea.

You will need:
Magazine photos of interesting characters
Wool tweed fabric or wrapping paper or gray, green, blue, or brown paper and crayons
Aluminum foil
Acetate or clear plastic wrap
Black construction paper

DIRECTIONS:

Reacquaint the class with the famous and formidable powers of Sherlock Holmes by reading them a passage from one of his cases in which he amazes Dr. Watson, his assistant, with his unbelievable deductions about the life and habits of a mysterious character. These passages occur in all the stories such as this passage from "The Red Headed League":

Our visitor bore every mark of being an average commonplace British tradesman, obese, pompous, and slow. He wore rather baggy gray shepherd's check trousers, a not over-clean black frock-coat, unbuttoned in the front, and a drab waistcoat with a heavy brassy Albert chain, and a square pierced bit of metal dangling down as an ornament. A frayed top hat and a faded brown overcoat with a wrinkled velvet collar lay upon a chair beside him. Altogether, look as I would, there was nothing remarkable about the man save his blazing red head and the expression of extreme chagrin and discontent upon his features.

Sherlock Holmes' quick eye took in my occupation, and he shook his head with a smile as he noticed my questioning glances. "Beyond the obvious facts that he has at some time done manual labor, that he takes snuff, that he is a Freemason, that he has been in China, and that he has done a considerable amount of writing lately, I can deduce nothing else."

Mr. Jabez Wilson started up in his chair, with his forefinger upon the paper, but his eyes upon my companion.

"How in the name of good-fortune, did you know all that, Mr. Holmes?" he asked. "How did you know, for example, that I did manual labor? It's as true as gospel, for I began as a ship's carpenter."

"Your hands, my dear sir. Your right hand is quite a size larger than your left. You have worked with it, and the muscles are more developed."

"Well, the snuff, then, and the Freemasonry?"

"I won't insult your intelligence by telling you how I read that, especially as, rather against the strict rules of your order, you use an arc-and-compass breastpin."

"Ah, of course, I forgot that. But the writing?"

"What else can be indicated by that right cuff so very shiny for five inches, and the left one with the smooth patch near the elbow where you rest it upon the desk?"

"Well, but China?"

"The fish that you have tattooed immediately above your right wrist could only have been done in China. I have made a small study of tattoo marks and have even contributed to the literature of the subject. That trick of staining the fish's scales of a delicate pink is quite peculiar to China. When, in addition, I see a Chinese coin hanging from your watch-chain, the matter becomes even more simple."

Mr. Jabez Wilson laughed heavily. "Well, I never!" said he. "I thought at first that you had done something clever, but I see that there was nothing in it, after all."

Now, show students a large photograph of an interesting character from a magazine and ask them to make a few deductions of their own. Encourage them to stretch their imagination and to be inventive, maybe even a bit outrageous. Hopefully, each student's comments will inspire others. When the class seems familiar with the deductive process, show them another character photo and have each student write a short paragraph of his or her own creative deductions. Cover the board with a tweed cloth or tweed printed paper, or have students create a simulated herringbone pattern on a conservative English color such as gray, brown, muted blue, or green. Use a yardstick and pencil to draw vertical lines on the paper, then dark- and light-colored crayons to draw diagonals between the stripes, as shown. Copy the magnifying glass and use aluminum foil, black paper, and acetate or clear plastic wrap to make the frame, handle, and glass more realistic. Place the large paper magnifying glass in the center of the board so that the character photo shows through the acetate "glass." Cut letters from foil to spell the title "Brilliant Deductions" and attach those to the board. After the bulletin board has been up for a few days, replace the photograph and have the class repeat the assignment. Later, students can create a mystery involving the characters they have deduced.

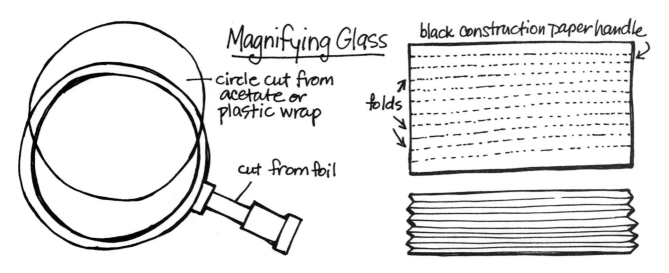

MONDRIAN MATH

Add an aesthetic flavor to a geometry class or a touch of mathematics to art by combining abstract art and geometric principles with this bulletin board idea.

You will need:
Tempera paint
Removable masking or cellophane tape
Black paper to cover the bulletin board
Rectangular white paper (suitable for tempera painting)

DIRECTIONS:

Surprise students in math class by discussing the Dutch abstract artist Piet Mondrian. He lived from 1872 to 1944 and painted as a Symbolist until he was influenced by Cubism. He achieved his greatest fame when he reduced his paintings to straight lines and rectangles and painted in the most basic, bright primary colors. Op artists, such as Victor Vasarely and Briget Riley, carried abstraction one step further and used carefully measured lines, shapes, and colors to create optical illusions. Look at some examples of these and other abstract artists' work. Then, ask students to use pencils, compasses, protractors, and rulers to create their own abstract art on paper.

You may wish to add specific geometric elements each student should include according to the geometric principle you are studying, such as a circle with a 2" radius, a 5" diameter, or a circumference of 3π, an isosceles triangle, or a trapezoid. Whether you are teaching the elements of one- or two-point perspective so that students can create an optical illusion that appears to recede in space or simply are allowing students to create, the only stipulation is that they must not draw freehand and must use the drawing instruments provided. When students have finished drawing their abstractions, they should be painted with bright colors and black and white to emulate the abstract artists' style.

Measure and cut a piece of solid black paper and use masking tape or cellophane tape applied horizontally and vertically to mask off rectangles and squares. Be certain to use a variety of tape that can be removed from the paper later. It is a good idea to test it on a sample sheet. Use small pieces of tape to write the words "Mondrian Math" as shown. Paint in the exposed squares with bright colors. Then, carefully remove the tape as soon as possible—before the paint dries completely. Place this paper on the bulletin board once it has dried; then add the students' artwork inside the rectangular divisions.

Apply masking tape.

Paint in rectangles.

Remove tape.

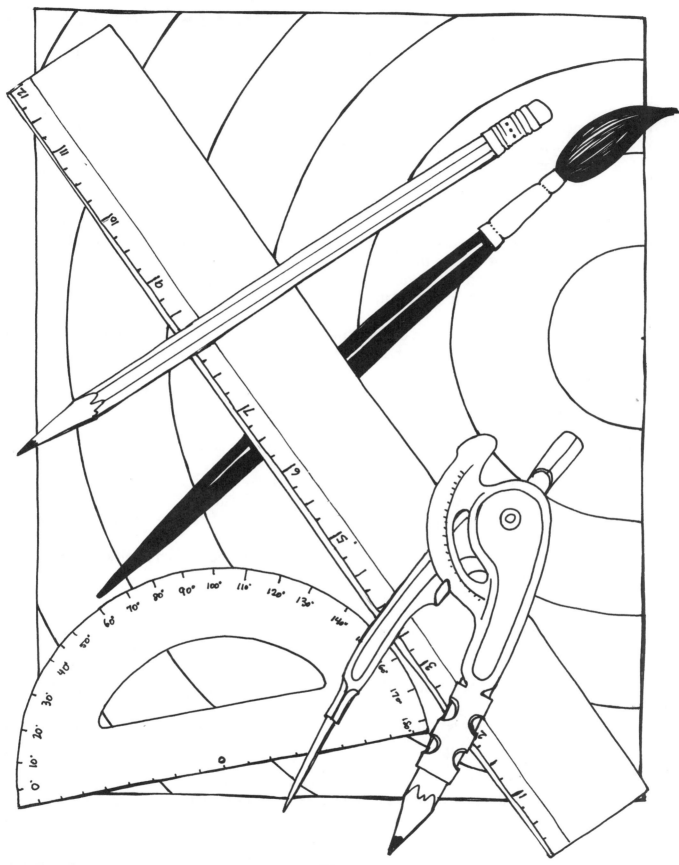

MATH HAPPENS

Suppose for a moment that you teach a class of students who do not intend to become mathematicians, architects, accountants, or math teachers. Why is it important for them to study math? This bulletin board offers some answers to that question.

You will need:
> White paper to cover the bulletin board
> Black and brightly colored construction paper
> Markers

DIRECTIONS:

Ask students to brainstorm about the ways they and their families use calculations in their everyday lives from the minute they get up in the morning. Appoint a fast writer to keep track of students' ideas on the board. The list may look something like this:

> Alarm rings, set at time calculated by hour school begins minus time required to prepare for it
> Shower time allowed based on total time divided by number of dirty family members
> Dress in clothing purchased based on total amount of dollars allowed for school clothes
> Breakfast on measured quantities of edibles selected from the various food groups according to optimal calories required for good nutrition
> At school, how many words have you written in your theme?
> How many points must your team score to win in gym class? Is the game divided into halves, quarters?
> How many years ago did the Civil War take place?
> How many average students does it take to fill an allosaurus?
> In what proportion should water be mixed with plaster of Paris to achieve the desired consistency?
> How many hours and minutes until supper? Is there time enough to pick up a friend and visit the mall?
> Do I have enough cash to buy a CD?
> How many video games can I afford to play before I run out of funds?
> How many weeks must I save my allowance to afford those athletic shoes?
> How much time can I spend on homework for each class to finish before bedtime?
> How far ahead should I begin the semester project so I will not have it all to do at the last minute?
> Can I go to the movies this weekend and still buy the T-shirt I want? What about pizza later?
> What size do I need? How do I measure myself?
> How do I figure out how much paint I need to paint my room?
> How long will it take me to walk to the park, and when should I leave to be on time to meet my friend?

Offer a few suggestions of your own if students have trouble coming up with ideas at first. Continue until you have at least one idea for each student in your class. Cover the bulletin board with solid white paper and add 6" squares of black construction paper with corners touching to achieve a checkerboard pattern. Cut a large yellow circle and place it in the center of the board. Surround it with red and orange triangles radiating from the center to form a sun. Cut blue or purple construction paper letters for the title "Math Happens" and place them above and below the sun. Cut out large numbers from 1 to 12 and place these around the sun's face as they would be on the face of a clock. Have each student write an idea the class has brainstormed on a brightly colored construction-paper triangle and place it somewhere on the sun or the checkerboard background. Add and subtract ideas over the coming weeks.

NO PROBLEM

Recycle the old "problem of the week" in this new format that is as intellectually exciting as it is stimulating.

You will need:
> White paper for background
> Black construction paper
> Brightly colored construction paper or printed gift wrap with no white in the design
> Black markers

DIRECTIONS:

At the beginning of the math period each day, or perhaps once a week, read the class a tricky math problem. You may wish to select these from the bonus problems in the current chapter of your text so they will be related to the topic being studied, or you may wish to keep the students on their toes with unrelated problems. These problems should be more difficult than the usual problems and involve looking at creative solutions as well as being careful not to be caught in traps of assumed expectations. After you have presented the problem to the class, write it on a small square of colored paper with the solution on the reverse side.

Cover the bulletin board with white paper and cut out black construction paper letters for the title "No Problem." Use bright colors of construction paper or rich, colorful gift wrapping paper to form huge numbers, large enough to almost cover the background. You may have to adjust the height or width of the example depending on the proportions of your bulletin board. Attach the letters and numbers to the bulletin board, as shown. Attach the problem of the week you have copied onto one of the large numbers, fastening it only at the top so that it can be lifted like a flap to reveal the solution. Keep track of who correctly answers the problem first. Have students take turns finding challenging problems.

A poor, lowly worm wasn't watching where he was going and fell down a well that was 20 feet deep. He began crawling out. It took him one day to inch 3 feet up the wall, but he slipped back down 2 feet that night. At this rate how long will it take the worm to crawl out of the well? Gulp!

Answer:
Well, well, well.
He gains one foot each day but he reaches the top of the well at the end of the 18th day, and, of course, he won't slide back down that night. GOOD THING there was no water in the well!

HARD ROCK

Most young people enjoy picking up various types of rocks they encounter on vacation or along the roadside. Many have started collections and studied rocks on their own. Beginning with this interest, increase the entire class's knowledge of geology with this bulletin board idea.

You will need:
> Brown paper bags or brown or gray paper
> Black, brown, and white crayons
> Rock and mineral identification guide book
> Black paper for background
> White paper

DIRECTIONS:

Prior to beginning this bulletin board activity, ask each member of the class to bring in an interesting rock or two. If anyone has a rock collection ask him/her to share it with the class. Otherwise, a specimen picked up on the way to school will do. Set aside some time for the class to examine these samples and pool knowledge. Have a rock and mineral identification guide on hand to look up puzzling items. Next, have students, working individually or in small groups, select a topic such as those suggested below to explore further:
> Rocks
> Petrology
> Lithosphere
> Asthenosphere
> Igneous Rocks
> Sedimentary Rocks
> Metamorphic Rocks
> Earth's crust
> Plate tectonics
> Minerals
> Gems
> Ore
> Crystals
> Amber, Coral, Pearls, Jet
> Continental Drift
> Divergent, Convergent, and Transform Fault Boundaries
> Paleomagnetism
> Volcano
> Magma, Lava
> Hawaiian, Strombolian, Vulcanian, Vesuvian, and Peléean
> Seismic Waves
> Earthquakes, Epicenter
> Caves, Caverns
> Stalactites, Stalagmites, Elictites, Columns
> Spelunkers

Students should prepare short paragraphs with appropriate illustrations of their findings. Cover the bulletin board with black paper. Tear brown paper bags open so that they lay flat and crumple them tightly; then spread them flat again. Using the flat edge of a black crayon which has the wrapper removed, color over the crumpled paper to create a stone effect by accentuating the creases. Repeat the process with dark brown, gray, rust, and ochre crayons to enhance the beauty and realism of the "stones." Tear some of the finished paper to form the letters for the title "Hard Rock" and attach them to the center of the bulletin board. Use additional torn pieces around the edge of the board to create a cavelike border. Have students place their paragraphs around the title after they have shared their information with the class.

cut bag

crumple

smooth flat

rub with crayon side

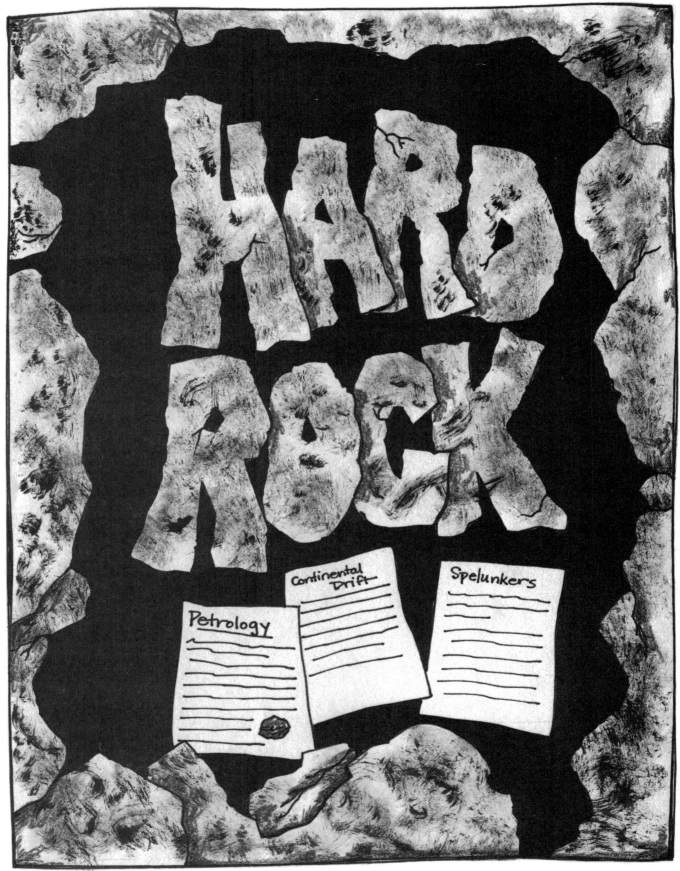

Ogling "Ologies"

This quick and easy bulletin board idea will alert students to the meanings and origins of words while providing an overview of the many, many different fields of scientific study.

You will need:
    White background paper
    Black construction paper
    Fluorescent colored paper
    Black markers
    Clear acetate

DIRECTIONS:

Start with a class discussion of the word *biology*. If the class is uncertain about the meaning, tell them that *bio* means "living" and *ology* means "study of." Using this information, have students guess the meanings of several other easy "ologies," such as zoology or geology. Next, have each student choose a new "ology" from the list provided (you may have some interesting ones of your own) and research the definition. Have each student write the "ology" on a circle cut from fluorescent paper. Use more fluorescent paper along with markers and sheets of acetate to make test tubes of various shapes containing strange scientific concoctions, as shown. Attach the test tubes along the bottom of the bulletin board. Have students explain the meaning of their "ology" to the class before they place their circles on the board to represent bubbles rising from the tubes. Add a few more smaller circles to fill in the gaps. Cut letters to spell the title "Ogling Ologies" from black construction paper and place them across the top of the bulletin board.

Once students have been introduced to the various fields of scientific study, you may wish to ask them to choose that field which interests them the most for further exploration.

A sampling of "ologies":
- Biology
- Paleontology
- Geology
- Cytology
- Gemology
- Speleology
- Physiology
- Embryology
- Ecology
- Mycology
- Entomology
- Bacteriology
- Sociology
- Oncology
- Archeology
- Anthropology
- Philology
- Dendrochronology
- Meteorology
- Topology
- Technology
- Cosmology
- Palynology
- Paleozoology
- Micropaleontology

And there are exceptions to every rule:
- Astronomy
- Botany
- Geography

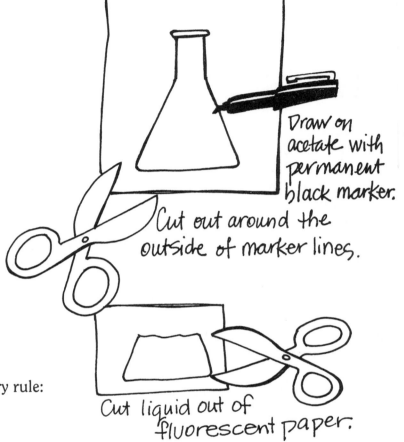

Draw on acetate with permanent black marker.

Cut out around the outside of marker lines.

Cut liquid out of fluorescent paper.

Fluorescent paper goes underneath acetate.

DINOMANIA

Human interest in those gigantic monsters that roamed the earth before us may wax and wane, but it never seems to disappear entirely. With new paleontological discoveries and recent motion picture releases utilizing cutting edge animation technology, it is no surprise that Dinomania is on the rise. Bring yourself and your class up to date on this prehistoric subject with this bulletin board activity.

You will need:
> *Jurassic Park* video
> Recent articles from magazines such as *National Geographic, Time,* and *Newsweek*
> Recent videos of television specials about dinosaurs, often available in the library
> Recent dinosaur books (with illustrations)
> Large brown paper
> Black crayons or markers
> White chalk
> Watered-down white glue
> Multi-colored tissue

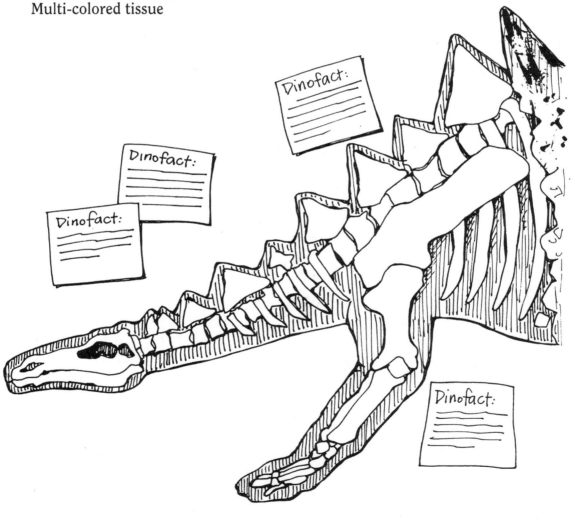

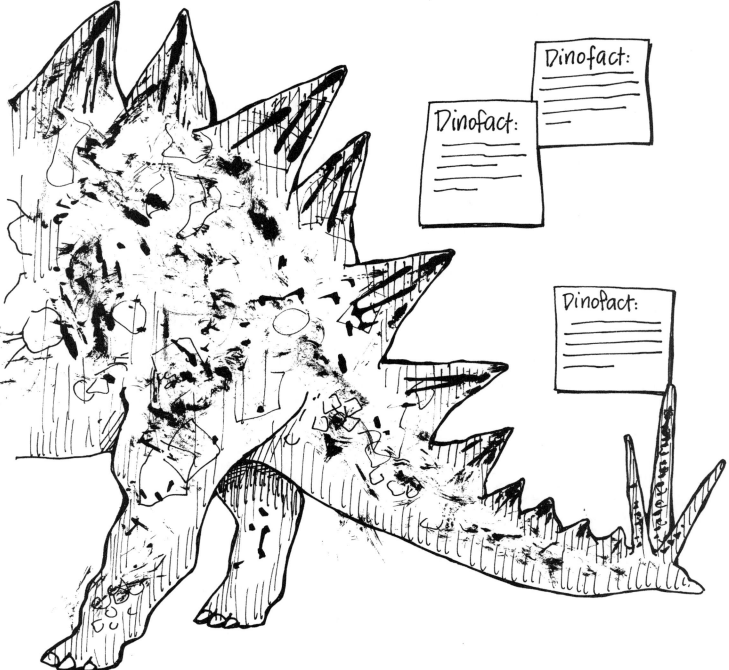

Dinofact:
_____
_____
_____

Dinofact:
_____
_____
_____

Dinofact:
_____
_____
_____

DIRECTIONS:

A slick way to begin this bulletin board activity is to show the video *Jurassic Park* or another recent video about dinosaurs. Though the movie is fiction, it was meticulously researched and based on the best and most recent "dinofacts." Take a few minutes to separate the fact from the fiction and discuss additional knowledge students may have about dinosaurs. Though much is known about the size, shape, and even the behavior of dinosaurs from fossil evidence, the actual coloration of dinosaurs is unclear because, of course, dinosaur hides do not survive in fossils. We can look to the animals most closely related to dinosaurs for clues—the reptiles and the birds. This opens up a brilliantly colorful world of possibilities, as these animals span the spectrum with spots, dots, stripes, and patterns of color. In his sequel to *Jurassic Park*, entitled *The Lost World*, Crichton even introduces a dinosaur species (Carnotaurus) that changes color like a chameleon. Octopi also change color rapidly and seem to melt into the background, so this ancient dinosaur species could have existed!

On the largest sheet of gray or brown paper available and in the largest space available in your classroom or hallway, copy the dinosaur illustrated in this unit, or have students draw the dinosaur of their choice. Note that the front of the dinosaur shows just the bones while the hind is in flesh. Once the animal is completed in pencil and mistakes have been erased, redraw all lines with black crayon or marker. Use white chalk to color in the skeleton portion and create the textured skin as follows: Lay torn pieces of tissue paper over textured surfaces (snake skin belts, radiator grates, rough wood, tires and soles of athletic shoes) and rub with the sides of black crayons, from which the paper wrappers have been removed. Apply a thin layer of thinned white glue to a section of the hind portion of the dinosaur drawing. Lay the desired color of textured tissue scrap over the glued area and apply more glue over the tissue. Add additional layers of tissue to create stripes, spots, and patterns of coloration as desired. The tissue will bleed and overlapping colors will blend, creating new colors. When the completed dinosaur has dried thoroughly, cut it out and staple or tape it to the display area. Use the same technique and leftover textured tissue to make the title "Dinomania" and affix it near the dinosaur. Have students each write a single fact they have learned from their studies of recent information about dinosaurs. Once they have shared their facts with the class, they can place them around the dinosaur. The first students to complete their fact sheets will be the first to present them to the class. Later students may not repeat a fact which has already been presented; they must discover a new fact.

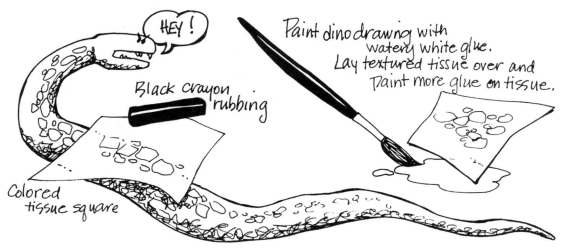

Clichés Are Overused

These have been called picture-words, word-pictures, riddle-words, and picture puzzles. But whatever they are called, they are lots of fun to create and fun to solve. Even more important, they also encourage creative thinking. Tickle your students' creativity centers and their funny bones at the same time with this bulletin board idea.

You will need:
> Markers (fine tip) or colored pencils
> Heavy white paper cut in 6" squares
> Construction paper, assorted bright colors, cut in 7" squares
> Black broad tip marker

DIRECTIONS:

Begin by drawing on the board a picture word that you have invented for students to guess. Or, make copies of the examples given here for each member of the class and give them a few minutes to figure them out. Once they know what each picture word means, have them explain the logic (or lack of it) behind its design. Have each student create one of his/her own and illustrate it using markers or colored pencils on a 6" square of white paper. The answer should be written in the center of a 7" square of brightly colored construction paper which has been stapled behind the completed picture puzzle so ½" shows around the edge like a frame. Cover the bulletin board with white paper and have a few members of the class use brightly colored markers to draw question marks of various sizes and colors over the entire surface. Write the picture word title "Clichés Are Overused" (as illustrated), using a thick black marker and a different bright color of construction paper for each letter. When each letter is cut out, leave ¼" of color showing around each black letter. Attach the title letters to the bulletin board and surround it with students' picture words. Once the bulletin board is complete, give each student's picture word a number; then have students number a sheet of paper correspondingly and see how many of the picture puzzles they can figure out. The first one finished gets the special question headband, a dubious honor!

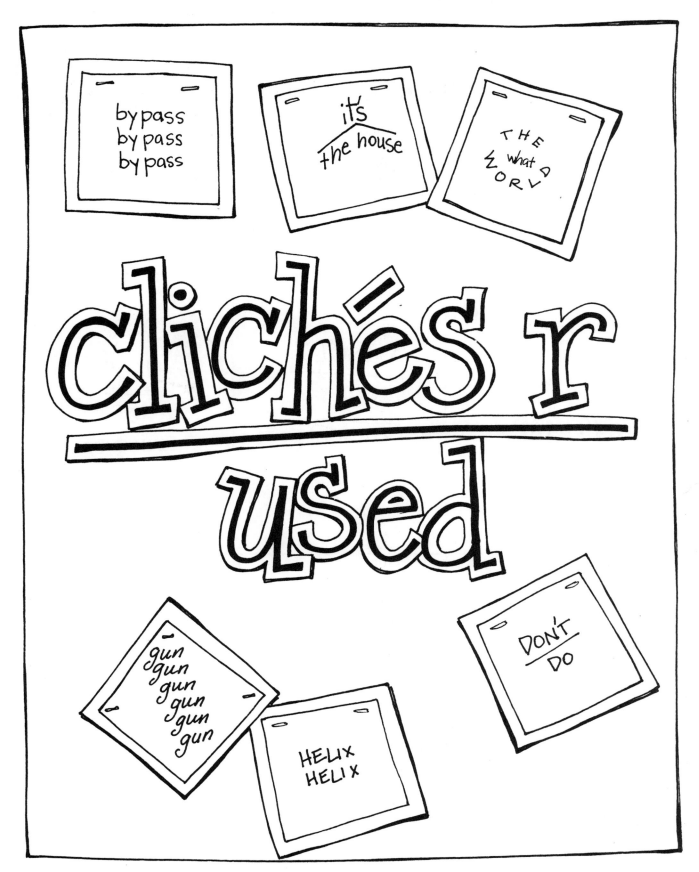

THE $_{WHERE}$ WORLD	BYPASS BYPASS BYPASS	she's her best. behavior
it's the HOUSE	WARMED —— LEFT —— SUPPER	DON'T —— DO
BUDGET △	ME AL ME AL ME AL	HE'S —— COME EMOTION

Left to right, top to bottom: Where in the world, triple bypass, she's on her best behavior, it's on the house, warmed over left-over supper, don't overdo, balanced budget, three square meals, he's overcome with emotion

© Instructional Fair • TS Denison

IF2550 Middle School Bulletin Boards

Math Hurricane's	*LOVE* (triangle)	gun gun gun gun gun gun
one the other one the other one the other one the other one the other one the other	HELIX	STOMACH
A N D O U T	friend JUST friend	PILF

Left to right, top to bottom: Hurricane's aftermath, love triangle, six-gun, half a dozen of one, half a dozen of the other, double helix, upset stomach, down and out, just between friends, backwards flip

THE REAL STORY

The way almost any story goes depends entirely on the point of view of the person telling the story. We are all familiar with eye witnesses who give totally different accounts after having seen the exact same incident. This bulletin board activity is based on the idea of personal perspective and perhaps will help students learn that we must be very careful not to believe everything we hear before we listen to both sides of a story.

You will need:
> Brown paper grocery bags
> Black and brown crayons, peeled, or black and brown tempera paint
> White drawing paper
> Markers or colored pencils
> Black construction paper
> Aluminum foil
> Magazines for clipping
> Newspapers

DIRECTIONS:

Begin the class by reading the picture book, "The True Story of the Three Little Pigs," by Jon Scieszka and illustrated by Lane Smith. This humorous story, told from the wolf's point of view, tells us what actually happened in the age-old fairy tale, insisting that he was a poor innocent wolf who was framed just because he was trying to borrow a cup of sugar to bake a birthday cake for his dear, sweet granny. Follow the reading of the story with a good-natured discussion of how we could have misinterpreted other fairy tales we know and love from our childhood. After all, Goldilocks' behavior could be thought of as "breaking and entering," and who would want to marry a prince who promised to kill you if you did not spin a whole roomful of straw into gold? Have each student take his/her favorite fairy tale, look at it from another perspective, and then rewrite it from this new point of view. Encourage students to be as outrageous as possible, and have them include one illustration of their story.

The stories should be typed or written in columns and glued to the front page of your local newspaper, with the story's title cut out of headline-type letters and glued into place. Mount the art onto the paper over a photograph so that the finished stories appear to be newspaper articles. Have 18 students each take a letter of the title "This Is the Real Story" and copy the letters shown in this unit, those in the back of the book, or create new ones. Cover the bulletin board with flattened and crumpled brown paper bags which have been colored lightly with the side of black and brown crayons or lightly sponge painted with black and brown tempera paint to create texture. This will simulate the prison wall in the story. You may wish to add a small black window made of black construction paper with gray bars cut from gray paper or aluminum foil. Attach the title letters to the bulletin board above the barred door, and place students' art work and true stories around them. Be certain to give each student the opportunity to read his/her story or plead his/her case, just as Alexander T. Wolf has done.

THE REAL STORY

SLIPPER SHATTERS CINDERELLA SLICED
Bloody scene disrupts ball
Royals repulsed

BEARS' BURGLAR APPREHENDED
The door was open says fair-haired felon

ROYAL DIVORCE!
Broasted bugs for breakfast bring break-up
I can't help myself!

Crumple, Smooth

Color with side of black and brown Crayons

or dab Crumpled and Smoothed paper with Sponge dipped in tempera

The Daily News

CAN'T A TROLL GET A DECENT NIGHT'S SLEEP?

"Each time I doze off, I'm awakened by an infernal "TRIP, TRAP, TRIP, TRAP"

Tyrone Troll was arrested late this afternoon for assault after he attacked not one but all three of the Gruff brothers, well-known billy goats in the area.

"We were just seeking the greener grass across the bridge," stated Big B. G. Gruff, who managed to fend off the troll's attack.

But Tyrone maintained that he had asked the three several times nicely to cross his property quietly. Trolls as we know, are nocturnal creatures and must sleep during daylight hours.

"I was so tired I just wasn't thinking straight," Troll responded to the charges leveled against him. "After all," he continued, "How would you like that constant disturbance?"

VOLUPTUOUS VOCABULARY

The older we get, the more often we find ourselves lamenting the fact that our students just do not have an adequate vocabulary. Though none of us uses the same English that was used in Shakespeare's day—most of those words have become archaic—new words are added to our language every day to describe inventions, objects, movements, and feelings that did not exist even a generation ago. Nevertheless, it is important to improve our vocabulary. This bulletin board idea serves two purposes—it improves vocabulary and students' creativity at the same time, all while making a game of it!

You will need:
> Glossy photographs from magazines
> Dictionaries
> White paper and markers
> Yarn, assorted colors

DIRECTIONS:

Have students collect glossy photographs from magazines (avoiding those with a lot of white in the background) and cover the bulletin board with them. Make certain the edges are torn rather than cut, and overlap the pages so that the entire board is filled in. On a white strip of paper, write "Vocabulary," and on another, write a word beginning with "V" that describes "vocabulary," such as *voluptuous*, *venerable*, *vicious*, *versatile*, or *vicarious*. Place the two strips of paper with the "v" words on them across the top of the bulletin board. Before the class begins, choose an unfamiliar word from the dictionary. Have the class look up the word and read the definition together. Note the type of information the dictionary tells us about each word, such as its phonetic spelling, meaning, part of speech, origin, and how it is used in a sentence. Now have the class put the dictionary away. Select another word and use a black marker to write it on a sheet of white paper attached to the center of the bulletin board. Ask each student to write a creative definition for the new word making it as convincing as possible using information similar to that given in the dictionary entries. Each definition should be written out on a small square of paper and may include a line art illustration, such as those that occasionally appear in the dictionary. Prepare one entry which has the correct definition and information.

Arrange all the entries on the bulletin board around the word and thumbtack colored yarn from the word to each definition. When all the definitions are in place, read them aloud and have students vote for the one they think is correct. Then, check the dictionary to see whether or not they have chosen the right one. Remove the yarn from the others. Vote again, on the most creative definition. When you are ready for a new word, change the "v" descriptor of "VOCABULARY" and select a new word for the center of the bulletin board. At the end of the year, give a venerable, voluptuous, vicious vocabulary test!

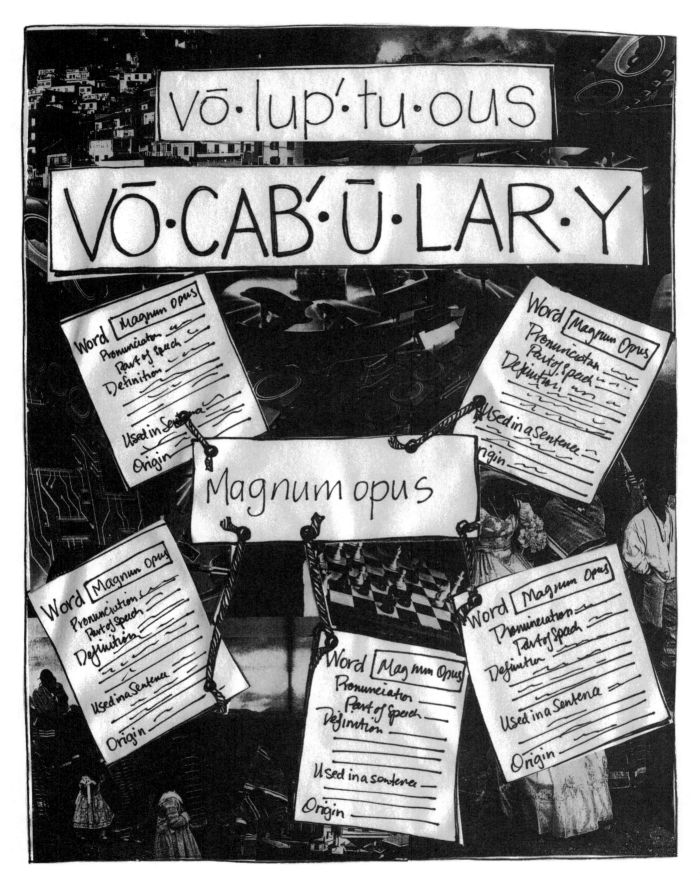

To make the process easier for students, you may wish to copy the following page and have students fill in the blanks.

Word
Pronunciation _____
Part of speech _____
Definition _____
_____
_____
_____
_____

Used in a sentence _____
_____
_____
_____

Origin _____
_____

LINK THINK

Long before children enter kindergarten, they become adept at naming similarities and differences in the world around them—things that fly, things that are alive, things we eat, things we wear, and games we play. Just when they think they have their world figured out and categorized, this activity comes along. It will warm up the brain cells as students stretch their imaginations to find commonalities in some rather uncommon pairs.

You will need:
> White paper to cover the bulletin board
> Purple or blue construction paper
> Thick yarn (greens, blues, turquoise)
> Paper clips
> Squares (2½" x 2½") construction paper

DIRECTIONS:

Choose two words. Make the two words fairly easy to connect, such as *dog* and *cat*. Begin by asking the class what these two words have in common. Once the easy commonalities are exhausted, i.e., both are pets; both have fur, tails, ears; both walk on all fours; both could be spotted, etc., ask students to think of more creative, obscure connections. Both animals frequently appear in Walt Disney movies, both have been domesticated from much bigger, more ferocious cousins, both can be taught tricks, both like to be petted and stroked, both come in many varieties and compete in pet shows, both are carnivores, etc. Encourage students to be as creative as possible in their responses, and also encourage humorous responses.

Now give students a list of six words and ask them to find a connection between each pair that they do not think any of their classmates will think of. Have them write their links on small squares (2½" x 2½") of construction paper. This could be a homework assignment.

Cover the bulletin board with white background paper, and cut out the letters of the title "Link Think" from purple or blue paper. Attach the letters to the board as shown. Cut six large oblong links from aluminum foil to represent chain links and place these around the title. Inside each link, attach a separate slip of white paper with one of the six words in the group written on it. Staple lengths of yarn from each word to every other word. Go around the class, asking each student to give one of the word links he/she has written on a square of paper, attaching it with a paper clip to the yarn that is stretched between the two linked words. As each student takes a turn, others in the class who have come up with the same link must throw theirs away. See how many different and unusual links the class can create. Repeat the process every so often, replacing the six words inside the links.

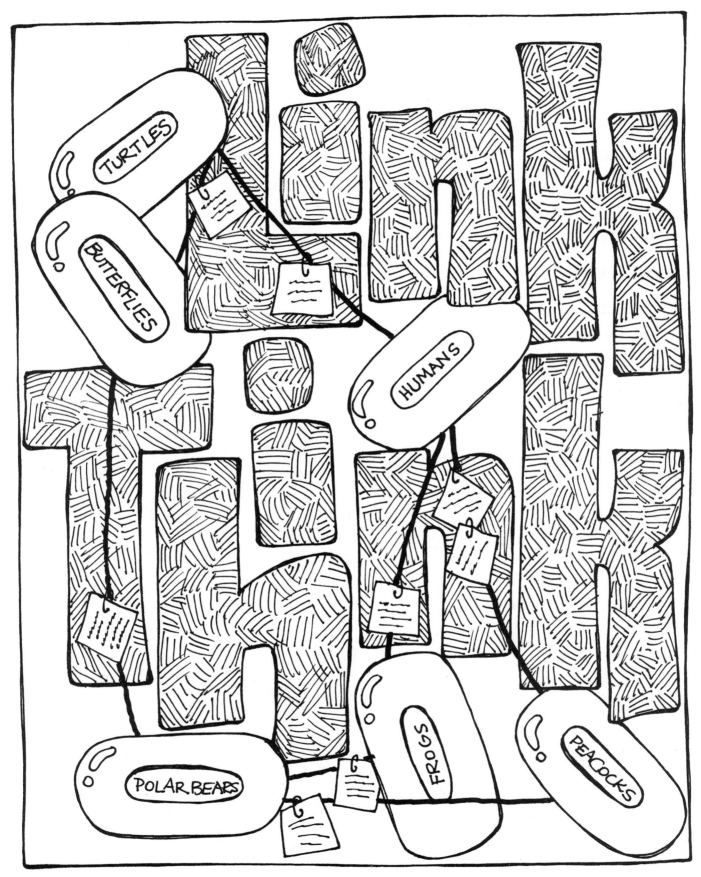

Blueberries
Holsteins
Ice cream cones
Water
Grubs
Mushrooms

Alligator
Plastic
Cotton plant
Sheep
Tractor
Trees

What possible connection is there between blueberries and Holsteins? I'll have to put on my thinking cap!

69

STRESS

Just like everyone else, middle school students today are facing more and more stress. This bulletin board idea offers a few suggestions to help them identify and to deal with it.

You will need:
    Bright solid color paper to cover the bulletin board
    White paper
    Bright or fluorescent crayons or markers
    Various shades of construction paper or fluorescent paper

DIRECTIONS:

Long ago, when our ancient ancestors had to flee from saber-toothed tigers or fight for their lives, their bodies developed physical responses to help them deal with these stressful situations. Adrenalin was pumped into their bloodstreams, giving them a shot of energy so that they could run a little faster or have strength so that they could fight a little harder and hopefully . . . survive! Though we do not often face fierce beasts these days, we do encounter lots of stress-filled situations with today's fast-paced lifestyle that our ancestors never dreamed of. Take a moment to discuss stress that occurs in our lives. Have students brainstorm about which specific things cause them to become worried or "stressed out." Have each student use a black crayon or marker to write out one of these "stress causers" onto a zigzag arrow which has been cut from bright construction paper. Use the pattern below, or have each student make his or her own individual zigzag for greater interest. Cut letters to spell the title "Stress" from white paper and add a zig-zag design to these letters with bright (even fluorescent) crayons or markers. Place the letters at irregular angles across the top of a bulletin board, which has been covered with any bright color. Copy the figure shown on the bulletin board, or have one student trace another's head, shoulders, and arms in a similar pose. Add eyes, mouth, and other details with crayons or markers, and place this figure at the bottom center of the board. Colored yarn may be added to make more interesting, textural hair. Add students' "stress causer" arrows around the figure, pointing to it.

EASING STRESS

After the stress bulletin board has been up for several days, change it into a DE-Stress board as students begin to search for possible ways to ease the tension in their lives.

You will need:
> White paper
> Markers or crayons
> Construction paper in pastel shades

DIRECTIONS:

Using the stress bulletin board as a visual aid, review the stress factors in students' lives. Now ask students to think of ways they could avoid, eliminate, or learn to deal with their stress. Look at each stress arrow individually and ask for suggestions about how that particular "stress causer" could be handled. Students will probably be able to offer suggestions to their classmates more easily than they can think of suggestions for solving their own problems because they can be more objective. Because prolonged stress, tension, and worry affect us physically, there are several things we can do to help our bodies cope with the physical effects of stress. These are the same things which, in general, promote good health:

> -Get plenty of sleep
> -Eat a healthy diet
> -Exercise regularly
>> Run, swim, skateboard, bike, play ball

Other stress relievers may be more specific, but may help a specific problem:

> -Dance and sing
> -Take up a relaxing hobby
> -Practice relaxation, breathe deeply
> -Close your eyes and count slowly
> -Talk to a friend; talk to yourself
> -Don't take yourself too seriously
> -Think of acceptable solutions in which everyone wins
> -Plan ahead to meet deadlines without stress
> -Study a little each night for three weeks before a big test
> -Practice your skill until it becomes second nature
> -Practice your music until you know it by heart

Use a magic marker to write "Easing" above the word "Stress" in a flowing script, or cursive, handwriting. Trace and color another student in the pose shown. This time, put a relaxed smile on his or her face. Now, have each student write out one of the stress-relieving suggestions on a small sheet of construction paper (soothing, pastel shades). Trim the edges so they are smooth and wavy and place them around the figure.

73

HUMOR IS HEALING

The old adage "Laughter is the best medicine" goes back a long way. People have always known that it makes us feel better when we laugh. Recent findings indicate that there is a physiological reason for this—laughter releases endorphins in our brains which are natural stress relievers. Some people even claim to have laughed themselves back to health from very serious diseases. Let laughter relieve some stress and improve the atmosphere in your classroom with this bulletin board idea.

You will need:
>   Dark paper to cover the bulletin board
>   White paper and fine tip markers
>   Colored comic section from the Sunday newspaper

DIRECTIONS:

Begin the class with a favorite joke of yours, or use this one.

A tourist visiting in the Middle East learned that wealth has long been measured by the number of camels someone owned. This seemed strange to the tourist because camels were not native to his land, but his interest was peaked and he decided he'd like to try riding one. The camel owner explained that riding a camel was simple. When you wanted to go, you whispered, "Phew" in the camel's ear and the camel would begin to walk. To speed up, say, "Phew, phew" and the camel would break into a run. To stop the beast, simply pull up on its tail. So the tourist mounted the camel and whispered, "Phew." The camel responded by moving forward. "This is great!" thought the tourist. After a little while the tourist was accustomed to riding and wanted to go faster. "Phew, phew," he whispered in the camel's ear and the animal took off running. With the wind in his hair, the tourist sped joyously across the sand, but soon he noticed that he was heading straight for a precipice at full speed. "Oh, what shall I do?" he cried, "I'm a gonner!" Then he remembered how to make the camel stop, so he quickly reached back and jerked up on the camel's tail. Just in time, the camel halted at the very brink of the precipice. As the tourist peered over the edge at the ravine far below, he was flooded with relief. Wiping his hand across his sweaty brow, he uttered, "Phew!"

Spend some time analyzing humor. What makes your students laugh? Many comedians poke fun at themselves, but jokes are in poor taste when they are told at the expense of others. Ask students to relate jokes they may have heard. Be certain that none of the jokes is insulting to any individual or group of people. Ask students if they feel each joke could offend anyone. Have each student find or invent one joke that they feel is very funny and write it on a sheet of paper. Cover the bulletin board with black or any other dark-colored paper. Have students cut out big letters from the color comics in the Sunday newspaper which spell assorted laughing words, such as *he, ha, ho, hilk, snort, chuckle, guffaw,* etc. Attach these letters at crooked angles all over the bulletin board. Have each student read his/her joke to the class; then add it to the board. Change the jokes any time you or a member of the class hears a good one. You can also have the class rate the joke on a laugh-o-meter as to its originality and political correctness. Maybe after students become experts on humor, they may write a few of their own jokes.

ACCENTUATE THE POSITIVE

Most people, and especially adolescents, tend to focus on their shortcomings and failures. Often because they feel insecure themselves, teenagers tend to make unkind remarks to one another which only serve to decrease self-esteem. Replace this negative tendency with the power of positive thinking in this bulletin board idea.

You will need:
> White paper to cover the bulletin board
> Black paper for title letters
> Brightly colored construction paper in contrasting colors
> White or colored stick-on paper labels

DIRECTIONS:

Ask students to think of some insults they may have heard on television or at school and jot them down on the board. Although words such as *stupid, worthless, ugly, liar, numb,* and other currently popular slang may seem funny, they serve only to belittle others and make them feel small. Label this list "Negatives." Now have the class think of words that instill confidence and increase self-worth and list these words under the heading "Positives." These would include such words and phrases as *caring, hard-working, smart, trustworthy, truthful, great athlete, beautiful smile, beautiful inside.* Ask students to take a minute to think about how they feel when someone uses a word from the negative list in reference to them. Ask the same about the positive list. Now, give each student a sheet of stick-on labels; ask each student to write the name of each member of the class in the corner of a label and one positive statement about that person. This can be done in class, or once the classmates' names have been copied, they may finish the labels at home so that they can give more thought to the matter and produce a more creative answer. Do not forget to include absent students. Students need not sign their positive labels, but they should put their names somewhere on the sheet of labels so that you can review them to make certain they are all positive.

Cover the board with a white background and cut out letters to spell the title "Accentuate the Positive" as shown. Make the over-sized accent marks a bright color and add funky designs. Have each student choose a bright color of 12" x 18" construction paper. Have equal numbers of sheets of red, green, orange, blue, yellow, and purple so that there will be a balance on the board. Fold the paper in half and cut a 3" strip off one side so that each student has a 9" x 18" piece folded into a 9" square. The three-inch strip should be traded with a classmate who has the complimentary color (opposites on the color wheel like red—green, yellow—purple, orange—blue). Have students use the scraps to cut out their initials and glue them onto their paper. They may also wish to add other colors of scraps cut in simple shapes to create an abstract design. When these designs have been completed, ask students to focus their eyes in the center of them and stare for 30 seconds. Then have them look at a blank sheet of white paper. The initials and design will appear on the blank paper as an after-image, only the colors will be switched! The negative after-image ties in with the positive/negative idea of the bulletin board. Place the cards on the bulletin board, attaching them at the top only so that the fold can be lifted. Return the positive sticker sheets to the students and have them stick each label to the appropriate student's card, under the flap.

You are lots of fun to be around.
Nice kind eyes.
I can count on you to tell the truth
You are always there to listen.
WOW

THE FAIR FIGHT

The classroom should be a safe, welcoming environment where learning can take place, but too often a lot goes on in the lives of students outside the classroom that disrupts the atmosphere within. This bulletin board idea identifies the components of facing conflicts in a way that is fair and may lead to a resolution of those conflicts. It also highlights words and actions that are unfair and only serve to escalate the conflict. Because the board accompanies a discussion and then remains in the classroom, the ideas are visually reinforced every day so that the fundamentals of fair play and getting along are reinforced.

You will need:
>	Light blue or white paper to cover the bulletin board
>	Mud
>	Yellow and brown construction paper
>	Markers

DIRECTIONS:

Conflicts arise wherever you go, whoever you are, and whatever you do. Human beings are constantly faced with conflict situations. There is just no escaping it. The important thing is to learn how to deal with it. Have students discuss some of the wrong ways of dealing with problems they may have seen others use or may have even used themselves. These are things, such as calling others names; mud-slinging or insulting others or their families; threatening them; pushing, shoving, fighting, or ignoring them; getting even by repeating the same wrong action back; and denying something or blaming someone else. Jot these ideas down on the board as they are introduced. Now ask students if they can think of better ways to handle a disagreement with another person, and jot these down as well. These may be a little more difficult to think of since we are more accustomed to the unfair methods (our politicians are very good at mud-slinging).

The "fair" list may include such items as stating exactly what the problem is and keeping the focus on that problem, speaking against the problem (not the person behind it), trying to keep an open mind, putting yourself in the other's shoes, owning up to something you have done, respecting a person's feelings, and stating your side in a nonthreatening way.

Cover half of the bulletin board with a bright color such as white or light blue and attach a big, yellow circle with a smiley face or the word "fair" or "yes" written inside it. Cut another sheet of paper to fit the other half of the board. Take it outside and stomp on it, smearing it with dirt and mud. When it dries, place it on the other side of the board with another circle at the top. This one should say "foul" or "no," or have a diagonal bar drawn through it. Have students share the task of copying the two lists from the chalkboard: the "good" ones should be written on curved sheets of paper resembling smiles, and the "bad" ones should be written on brown construction paper that has been cut in the shapes of splats of mud. These should be attached to the appropriate side of the bulletin board. You may wish to cut a few extra shapes so that additional "good" and "bad" suggestions may be attached later.

PEACE MAKERS

This bulletin board serves as an introduction to the techniques of mediation which may encourage some class members to become peacemakers in your school. But whether students are official mediators or not, knowing these techniques can help them in school and in life to settle issues fairly and peacefully.

You will need:
- Psychedelic print fabric or wrapping paper or blue background paper
- White paper for letters and peace symbol
- Black and colored markers

DIRECTIONS:

All of us, from young people to adults, from families to nations have to face and resolve conflicts. We may appeal to a higher power, such as a parent, teacher, or judge and jury to decide who wins and who loses, but a much better method is to have both parties sit down together and work out their differences so that everyone is satisfied and the conflict is resolved in a win/win situation. Civilized nations do this because the alternative can be very uncivilized—war! Those who successfully engage in this detente are truly great peacemakers. In schools, this process is sometimes called *mediation*. Students train in simple techniques to become the peacemakers of the school. Introduce these concepts to the class and go through the steps of a typical mediation process. The student mediators first listen impartially to both sides of the issue without passing judgment; then they ask those in conflict to suggest possible solutions to prevent the problem from arising again. They may have to suggest some solutions. All suggestions are then studied by those in conflict, and the best solution for both sides is selected and agreed upon. Last, the two in conflict are asked what they each could do differently in the future to prevent this from happening again. There are responsibilities that the disputants must also accept before the mediation begins: They must agree to work until the conflict is resolved, they must promise to tell the truth, they must fight fair (see bulletin board "The Fair Fight"), they must not interrupt when the other person is speaking, and they must carry out what they agree to do during the mediation session.

Cover the bulletin board with psychedelic print fabric or wrapping paper or use solid light blue. Use white paper to cut a peace symbol nearly as large as the board itself. This large circular shape can be made easily by tying one end of a string to a pencil and thumbtacking the other end to the center of the circle. The length of the string should be the radius of the circle. Hold the pencil upright and carefully pull the pencil around its center point. Reduce the length of the string by 4" and draw a concentric circle inside the first so that the ring is 4" wide. Cut a 4" wide template of oaktag on the paper cutter and draw the three bars inside the circle to complete the peace sign. Draw two more concentric circles outside the peace sign, one with a radius 1" larger than the sign and the other with a radius about 7" larger. Use these circles as the top and bottom edges for the letters of the title "Peace Makers." Cut out and attach the letters to the bulletin board as shown. Have students copy the rules of mediation onto small pieces of white paper and place them inside one of the divisions of the peace sign. In another division, place the steps of the mediation process. In the bottom wedge, add a dove of peace.

PEACE

Disputants'
Responsibilities
1. Work until solved.
2. Tell the truth.
3. Fight fair.
4. No interruptions.
5. Promise to follow
through on
solutions
agreed
upon.

Mediator's
Responsibilities
1. Listen to both sides.
2. Ask for solution sug-
gestions from disputants.
3. Help decide on best
solution.
4. Ask for suggestions
for future
prevention.

MAKERS

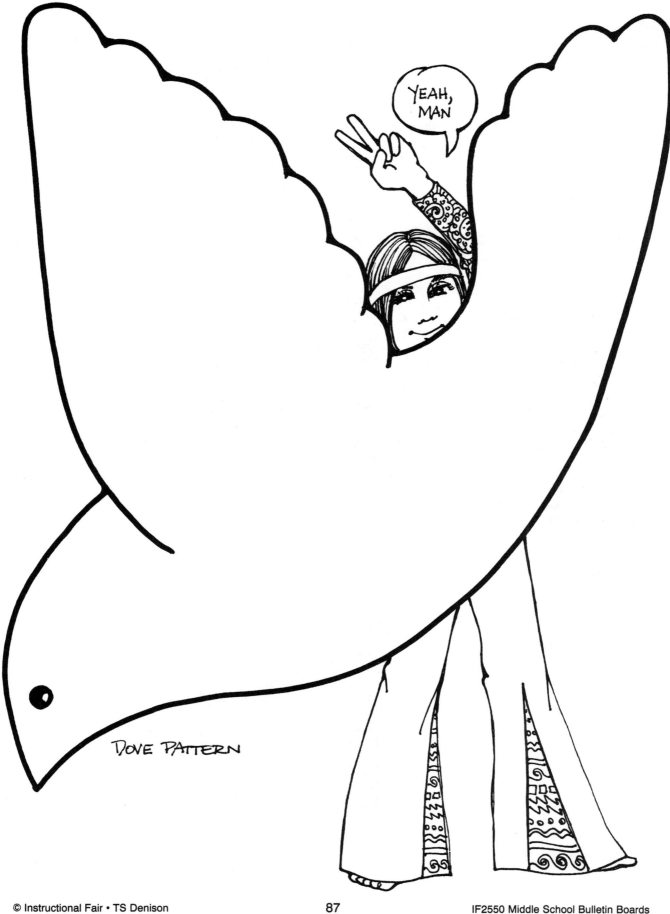

Dove Pattern

NURTURE OUR WORLD

One way in which we can show respect to others is to respect this small planet where we must all live together. This bulletin board idea helps us to understand this concept and teaches us some ways to enact it.

You will need:
      Paper and foil wrappers to cover the bulletin board
      Black markers
      White paper
      Blue construction paper or bulletin board paper
      Crayons or colored chalks
      Polyester fiberfoam

DIRECTIONS:

Write the capital letters "NOW" vertically on the board. The class, of course, knows the meaning of this three letter word. Next to these letters, complete the words, "Nurture Our World." Discuss the meaning of this phrase with the class. Be certain that students understand the concept that we must all take care of our small planet for our own health and the health and happiness of future generations. This means encouraging the clean-up of toxic waste; setting aside natural beauty areas; conserving fuels; searching for new, cleaner fuels; protecting endangered species; controlling our world's population; etc. Many of these practices are beyond the power of students, although they may make their opinions known to those in power. There are, however, many things students can do to show they care about their planet. Introduce the following facts to the class as well as others you or your students may have heard:
      -Each American generates four pounds of trash per day.
      -It is often easier and cheaper to recycle metal than to mine it.
      -Litter along the roadside and on our school's campus is unsightly and shows that
         we do not care how we live or what others think of us.
      -20% of trash by volume is plastic. Some companies are experimenting with
         this discarded plastic to make such items as flower pots and park benches.
      -The most common item in trash (40%) is paper, which could be recycled.
      -Yard waste (leaves and grass clippings) make up 18% of trash in landfills, yet if it is
         composted and returned to the garden, it improves the soil.
Many of the facts above come from free pamphlets available from the EPA (Environmental Protection Agency), which can be ordered by calling:
      Resource Conservation and Recovery Hotline
      1-800-424-9346
Or by writing:
      OSW Publications
      Office of Solid Waste
      U.S. Environmental Protection Agency
      401 M Street S.W.
      Washington DC 20024

Study these or other booklets and pamphlets about recycling and ask students to discover some trash problems and solutions of their own. Have them think of a few ideas that they could do for their community to give it a little TLC (tender loving care).

These suggestions should be written in black marker on white paper that has been cut in the shape of a capital T, L, or C. Try to get an equal number of each letter. Ask students to save clean paper, light cardboard, and foil wrappers from food they eat throughout the day, such as bottle, candy, and chip wrappers. Include wrappers of nonedible items also, such as soaps, pencil packaging, or toys. As students bring them in, use them to cover a bulletin board, overlapping them so that they form a solid background. Use black markers to write the title "Nurture Our World" on white paper, leaving a ¼" to ½" border showing around the letters, as shown. Attach the title at an angle across the top of the bulletin board. Cut a large blue circle to represent the earth, adding faint land masses with green, white, and brown crayon or colored chalk. Attach it to the board below the title and add a few wisps of cotton or polyester fiberfoam to represent clouds. Have each student share his/her idea with the class and place the TLCs in groups on the bulletin board around the pampered planet.

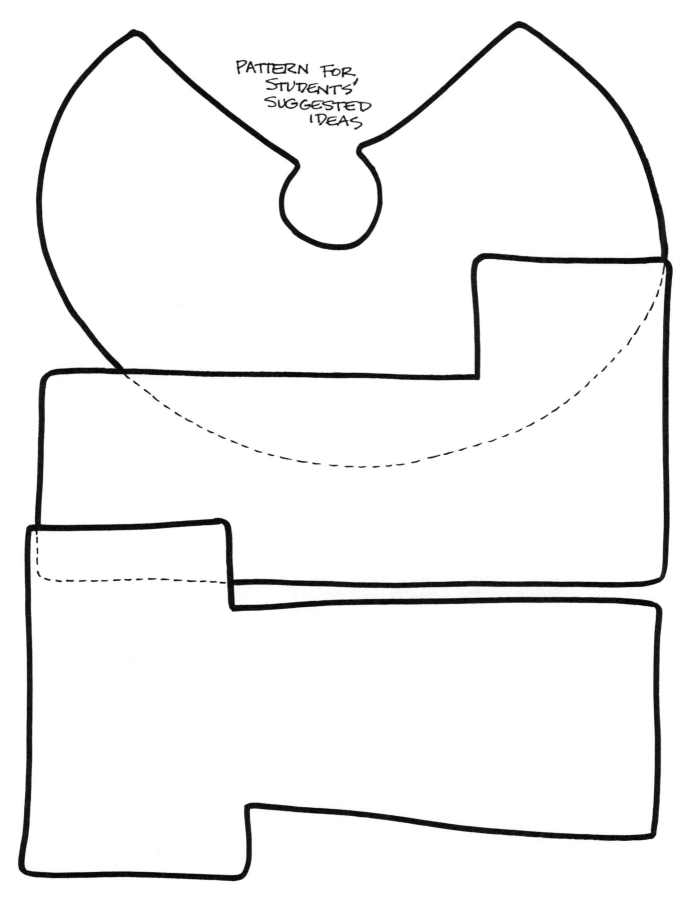

PATTERN FOR
STUDENTS'
SUGGESTED
IDEAS

RANDOM ACTS OF KINDNESS

In our fast-paced world, it seems we have little time to get to know people, much less treat them as friends whom we love and respect. Use this bulletin board activity to improve your community and your class's sense of community.

You will need:

      Dark soft fabric or paper to cover the bulletin board
      White, pink, baby blue, and yellow paper
      Pushpins
      Marker

DIRECTIONS:

Begin the activity with a discussion of what is meant by the word *community* and the phrase "community service." Ask students if they can remember an activity in which they participated with their family, class, or scout troop which performed a community service or another act of kindness. The act need not have been a major organized activity. Perhaps some students can remember a situation in which they did someone a favor or someone helped someone out. Did the experience make them feel good about themselves? Jot down students' offerings on the board. Then, ask the class for ideas they may have about some activities they may do as a class or individually during the school year. Some suggestions may be as follows:

      -Visit a nursing home.
      -Visit a preschool and teach a new game.
      -Hold a food drive for the needy in the community.
      -Collect clothing for a family who has suffered a fire.
      -Visit a shut-in.
      -Adopt a small plot of earth to clean up and plant flowers. Be certain to follow
          through with weeding and watering.
      -Volunteer at the library, art center, dog pound, public theater, or other nonprofit
          public facility in whatever capacity is needed.
      -Mow lawns or shovel sidewalks for shut-ins in your neighborhood.
      -Have each student take a mental walk down his/her street and think whether there is
          anyone living there who could use help in some small way.
      -Have students tour the neighborhood with trash bags, collecting any trash on the
          ground.
      -Write a personal letter to graduating seniors asking them not to drink and drive.
      -Make colorful get well cards and deliver them to hospital patients.

Contact local churches and community groups who may have some programs already in place to see whether they could use some extra pairs of hands. After the ideas have been suggested, have students choose activities they would like to pursue individually, in small groups, or as a class. Agree on a number of hours each student should donate and specific jobs to qualify. Some students may earn their hours making phone calls to line up volunteers or making posters or cards. Cover the bulletin board with a soft, dark fabric cut to fit from an old blanket or bedspread. Cut letters from yellow paper to spell the title "Practice Random Acts of Kindness." Make a second set of letters from pink for the word "Kindness" and baby blue for the word "Random." Place these on the bulletin board as illustrated, placing the pink and blue letters over the appropriate yellow letters so that the words appear shadowed. In the center of the board, place a white chart with a yellow border which lists all the students' names down the left side of the page and provides space to check off hours fulfilled in the kind service of others. Around the sides of the bulletin board, pin notes to update the class on the progress toward the goal, also noting any small acts of kindness any students have been caught practicing.

95

WISH YOU WERE HERE

Give students an overview of the past with this slightly different and hopefully humorous approach to history.

You will need:
> Light-colored paper to cover the bulletin board
> Black construction paper to shadow letters
> 6" x 9" stiff paper suitable for making postcards

DIRECTIONS:

Read the class the message from the accompanying sample postcard and ask them to guess who wrote it. They should be able to guess from clues in the message where and when this imaginary correspondence took place. Now have students choose a person, place, and time from the list that follows or coordinate selections with your semester plans. Have students research the lifestyle of the chosen time period and the events in the life of the famous character. Give each student a 6" x 9" piece of stiff paper to write an imaginary postcard from that time period similar to the example you read to the class. Stress that they should use a combination of the knowledge they have gained, plus their imagination and sense of humor. Some of the suggested characters, such as the cavemen, lived in a time before writing so some liberties will need to be taken. Perhaps some hieroglyphics could be included in the ancient Egyptian postcard. Be certain students write about something that could have occurred in their selected era based on their research. They should write on the left half of one side of the card and should create an address, postmark, and stamp appropriate to the era on the right side. It would be more realistic if the stamp were drawn, colored, and then glued on the upper right corner of the postcard.

On the other side of the postcard, have students glue an appropriate illustration either drawn by hand, cut from a magazine, or photocopied from a resource and colored. From black construction paper, cut letters to form the title "Wish You Were Here." Cover the bulletin board with a light-colored paper and attach the letters at an angle across the top. Have each student read his/her postcard to the class just as you read the sample so that the class can guess who, when, and where in time it was written. Show the picture on the front of the card for further clues. Finally, attach each postcard to the bulletin board with a pushpin or tack so that it can be removed and examined by students in their free time over the next few weeks. You may wish to draw a faint ambiguous postmark on the bulletin board with black crayon.

Dear Gramma,
    I am so exhausted these days I can
barely write. Each day we get up at dawn,
eat warmed up salt pork and beans, and
drink some strong coffee. Then we're on the
trail again. Pa drives the oxen, Ma usually
sits beside him tendin' little Seth, while
Jacob, Josh, and I walk alongside. The
prairie seems like a vast ocean, the land
rising and falling in soft swells, and
when the wind blows, the grass moves
like waves. Yesterday, we saw some
Indians way off in the distance, but they
didn't pay us no mind. Some clear days
we notice tiny, faint purple peaks on the
horizon. These, folks say are the Great
Rocky Mountains we've heard tell about.
Wish you were here, Gramma. Love Sarah.

Mrs. Clementine Munson
Main Street
Cleveland
Ohio
United States of
America

Examples from which students can choose:

- Caveman writing from scenic Lascaux
- Roman soldiers invading England
- Queen Bodecia fighting off the Roman soldiers
- Ancient Druids
- Workmen building Stonehenge
- Scots in kilts suffering chapped knees
- Ghengis Kahn
- James Cook discovering Australia in 1770
- Montezuma taking revenge
- Eric the Red or his illustrious son, Leif
- Robinhood
- Richard the Lion-Hearted
- Cyrano de Bergerac
- William Wallace
- An American pioneer crossing the prairie
- A robotic man of the future
- Christopher Columbus or other explorers of the period
- Queen Elizabeth
- Bloody Mary

THE DAILY NEWS

We read the newspaper and watch the evening news to keep ourselves informed of the world around us. Try this bulletin board activity to put an interesting slant on how we view the world.

You will need:
> Newspapers to cover the bulletin board
> Black construction paper
> Red, green, and blue fine line felt tip markers
> Blank white newsprint cut in 3" widths or yellow, red, and orange construction paper strips

DIRECTIONS:

Read an article of interest from your local newspaper to the class. Choose an article that is typical of common life occurrences in your part of the country. For example, in Maine a moose on the loose in a town makes local headlines, while a roving alligator may spark a story in Florida. Have students then write a short newspaper item of their own based on something of local interest that happened somewhere other than their hometown. They may find their story as an Associated Press item in the local newspaper, in a newspaper subscribed to in the library, or on the national news on television. These articles should be written in the style of a newspaper article with all pertinent information—who, what, when, where, why—written briefly in the first paragraph and elaborated on in subsequent paragraphs. Students should print their articles in small letters using red, green, or blue felt tip markers on 3" wide strips of paper to resemble a newspaper article. If students are working on computers, use 2½" margins and select colored ink, if available, to print them, or mount the finished article on colored paper. Cover the bulletin board completely with newsprint and cut out large black letters for the headline "The Daily News" as shown.

Attach these across the top of the bulletin board. Have students add their stories vertically over a newspaper column on the newspaper background once they have shared the article they have written with the class.

Using the same bulletin board, ask the class to write current events articles of global interest which they have read in the local paper, a weekly news magazine, or heard on any television newscast.

Use the same bulletin board to conduct your weekly current events discussion, adding clippings instead of stories, perhaps following one story in particular over the next few weeks.

The DAILY NEWS

Local News
Global Developments
Current Events

MOOSE ON THE LOOSE

SALT WATER INTRUSION PUTS FISH AT RISK

RODEO KING AND QUEEN CROWNED

FEAR OF AVALANCHE BUILDS WITH SNOWFALL

SCREAM FOR ICE CREAM

LEAF PEEPERS OUT IN FORCE

FUTURE SHOCKING

Mankind has always dreamed of how people would live in the future. Leonardo da Vinci imagined flying machines and Jules Verne dreamed of submarines in *20,000 Leagues Under the Sea*. See what your students can imagine in the future with this bulletin board activity.

You will need:

> Silver wrapping paper or aluminum foil to cover the bulletin board
> Fluorescent paper and black construction paper
> Assorted colored plastic bottle lids, square laminate samples, lightweight gizmos and gadgets
> Hot glue gun

DIRECTIONS:

Begin this activity by discussing movies, television programs, and science fiction books that members of the class may have seen or read which take place in the future.

These may include:

Back to the Future II

Terminator

Logan's Run

Soylent Green

2001 Space Odyssey

Blade Runner

Waterworld

Mad Max

Star Trek

Star Wars

The Jetsons

Dune

Planet of the Apes

Robot

Some of these may have portions which are not suitable for the class to see; nevertheless, they may have seen them. Ask students how believable these future stories are and why we like to believe them. The authors had to use clever combinations of science fiction and science fact to predict how humans and extraterrestrials would live their lives in the future. We find ourselves saying, "It's possible—it could happen." Life in the future is improved over life in the present in some of these stories, while in others, life is much worse. Some futuristic authors are real pessimists! How do students feel? Do they think the future will hold a better life for their children's children? Have each student try his/her hand at prediction and prepare a short paragraph about life in the future. They may choose to take a broad overview and discuss evolutionary changes in mankind (Kevin Costner had gills in *Waterworld*) or simply write about a day in the life of a middle school student in the year 3000, 4000, or 5000. The final copy of the paragraphs should be written on fluorescent paper cut into odd shapes, such as triangles, parallelograms, or anthropomorphic blobs. Cut a matching shape for each student from black construction paper. Cover the bulletin board with silver wrapping paper or aluminum foil and use black construction paper to cut out the letters to spell the title "Future Shocking." Place these letters vertically up the side of the board. You may also wish to cut an additional set of title letters from fluorescent paper and place them under the black letters so that a little of the bright color shows through and highlights the title. Add a 4" x 6" band of black paper across the bottom of the bulletin board and use a hot glue gun to stick colorful plastic lids, laminate samples, or other gizmos which resemble space age dials to the black band of paper. Glue extra gizmos to students' paragraphs, if desired. Take time for each student to read his/her paragraph to the class before placing it on the bulletin board. Do not forget to place the matching black shape under it slightly askew.

DOODLE A LITTLE DANCE

Dancing is as much an integral part of the human experience as is the heartbeat. Explore this kinesthetic art form with this bulletin board activity.

You will need:
>   White or light paper to cover the bulletin board
>   Heavy black marker
>   Assorted colors of construction paper or wallpaper samples for letters

DIRECTIONS:

Ask the class how many of them enjoy dancing. What is the current popular dance called? Do any of them know any dances their parents or grandparents did back in the "olden days"?
>   The Twist
>   The Monkey
>   The Mashed Potatoes
>   The Jerk
>   The Swim
>   The Jitterbug
>   The Charleston
>   The Waltz
>   The Minuet
>   The Samba
>   The Electric Slide
>   The Macarena
>   The Boogie Woogie
>   The Lucky Lindsey
>   The Bristol Stomp
>   The Tango
>   Square Dance

These are, or were, popular dances in our society, but they only scratch the surface of this form of human expression. There are dances requiring a lifetime of training, such as ballet, modern dance, tap, or jazz. There are classical dance forms around the world and ancient tribal dances that have great religious significance. But most people simply dance for the joy of moving their bodies to music. Find out more about this art form by having students work individually or in small groups. Have them choose one of the examples of dance listed above or others they may know to research. You may wish to limit the selections to popular dances of the twentieth century, classical dances around the world, folk dancing, the evolution of dance through time, or the religious significance of ancient tribal dances to Native Americans, Africans, or Australian Aborigines. Have each student or group prepare a short report complete with drawings, photographs from magazines, or photocopies. Cover the bulletin board with white or light paper and cut the letters for the word "Dance" from assorted interesting colors of construction paper or wallpaper samples. Place these letters at crooked angles across the bottom of the bulletin board as though they are dancing. Use a heavy black marker to write "Doodle a little'" across the top; scribbles, doodles, and musical notes down both sides; and draw arms, legs, and faces on the "dancing" letters. Have each student or group share research with the class before placing their reports on the bulletin board. Once students have become experts on dance, you may wish to view some videos of various dance forms. Perhaps some students will even volunteer to demonstrate some of the dances they know!

a Macarena!

REAL CHARACTERS

Sometimes the simplest method to teach sophisticated ideas is to use elementary examples. This bulletin board idea presents the concept of character development using a very friendly means—a Disney cartoon.

You will need:
> Solid red paper to cover the bulletin board
> Another bright color for the letters
> White paper
> Markers, crayons, or tempera

strict
prim
cruel
perfectionist
demanding
Teacher of the Year

DIRECTIONS:

Show the class a videotape of a Walt Disney movie such as *Bambi* or *The Lion King*. Ask students to keep a list of all the cartoon characters, their character traits, the emotions they think children are supposed to feel when they watch it, and the ways in which this characterization is achieved in the cartoon. These cartoons are great tools to use with older students because there is nothing subtle about them, making them easy to analyze. They are also fun! The "emotion" list should probably include *joy, despair, bravery, greed, evil, triumph over hardship*, etc. Disney uses background music, songs and lyrics, dialogue, exaggerated character body movements, facial expressions, colors, and background scenery to achieve desired results. You may want to stop the video occasionally to ask students their reactions. When the movie is finished, focus on the expressions in the faces of the characters and those features of each that make them good, evil, endearing, slimy, proud, or silly. Now ask each student to design a cartoon character of his/her own and to prepare a list of character traits the character exhibits. They may wish to draw from the multitude of Disney characters they have grown up with, characters from comic strips, super heroes, or their own imaginations. After they have made a few sketches, they should each make a finished drawing of the face or entire body of their creation, and, on a separate sheet, list the character traits that their character possesses. Cover the bulletin board with solid red or any other bright primary color and cut cartoon letters with black shadows as shown to spell, "Real Characters." Place the title whimsically across the top of the board and have students add their characters beneath. Do not post the list of character traits. Have the class guess what sort of character they think each student creation possesses first; then check the guesses with the list.

CREATIVE CONSPIRACY

Self-expression can take many forms—music, dance, poetry, prose, visual arts, athletics. A visual artist experiences feelings of elation and satisfaction when totally involved in his or her work. This feeling is not limited to the visual arts; it is common among musicians, dancers, athletes, writers, and also among those of us who enjoy these art forms as spectators. Humans elevate their spirits and touch one another's hearts by sharing themselves through the arts. That so many different people can be emotionally moved by such a variety of different art forms sometimes seems a great conspiracy of the arts. This bulletin board idea explores the many ways we are elevated by the arts.

You will need:
>   Samples of favorite artwork, music, poems, passages, moments in sports events, and dance
>   Construction paper in assorted colors
>   Markers or paints, paper and foil scraps, glue, scissors
>   Solid white or black background

DIRECTIONS:

Cover the bulletin board with solid white or black paper. Give each of 18 students a sheet of construction paper in different assorted colors and have them create letters to spell "Creative Conspiracy." Each letter should be unique, in a different typeface, and decorated with markers or glued-on paper or foil scraps. This could be a homework assignment so that students can take advantage of interesting items they may have at home. It can also be done in class with items brought from home as a fun and relaxing Friday afternoon activity. If you have fewer than 18 students in your class, double up on the letters, and if you have more, have them decorate strips to use as a border. Attach the finished letters to the bulletin board. Play a piece of your favorite music for the class. It may be classical, swing, blues, or rock—it does not matter. Ask students to close their eyes as they listen, and afterwards, tell them why you like it so much, how it makes you feel, what it reminds you of, etc. It may make you feel uplifted, terribly sad and filled with melancholy, patriotic, full of hope, or very angry. It may remind you of a time in your life when you felt the summer sun on your face and all was right with the world. Share your feelings with the class as creatively as possible. Ask several students to bring in their favorite music and be prepared to play it for the class. Then have them tell what they feel about their choice and why. Repeat this process with a piece of art work, a photograph (from a magazine), an excerpt from a novel or a poem, a video of a dance performance, a music video, or a great moment in sports. Any of these is acceptable so long as the student can explain why it moves him/her. Everyone should take a turn. As students share their "arts" experience with the class, they should also prepare a short visual presentation, a paragraph, an illustration, or a photograph to place on the bulletin board around the title.

This board involves a broad range of art forms, but the same idea could be repeated narrowing the focus to one of the following: poetry, passages from a book the class is studying, photographs from events around the world, or visual art that evokes strong emotions.

If you love somebody,
set them free.
To think and feel
and grow and be.
(from listening to Sting)

MAKING FACES

We all love to dress up in costumes and don masks which transform us into someone or something else at Halloween time. But this is just one example of the many functions human beings have invented for masks throughout history and around the world. Explore the art of masks with this bulletin board activity.

You will need:
> Black, royal blue, or purple velvet or paper for the background
> 12" x 18" oaktag for the letters
> Assorted mask-making materials, such as string, buttons, feathers, paint, shells, and beads

DIRECTIONS:

Ask students to identify the favorite mask they ever wore for Halloween or any other occasion. How did they feel when they wore it? Did their personality change and take on the character of the costume? Discuss other times and places students may have seen masks being worn and make a list of them on the board. Masks are used by:
> Africans performing ancient rituals
> Mardi Gras revelers
> Chinese opera performers
> Classical dancers of India
> Native Americans at tribal festivities
> Masked balls
> Ancient Greek theater
> Medieval festivals

Masks are worn for a variety of reasons. Greeks exaggerated the features on their masks so that expressions of the actors could be seen from far up in the back row. African masks were used in the celebration of major life events, such as the coming of age, death, and wedding ceremonies. Native Americans created masks in the image of animals to represent the spirits of animals. Chinese opera masks are highly stylized and represent specific character types that the audience recognizes. Masks have been made from just about every material imaginable: wood, paper maché, feathers, skins, paper, shells, beads, hair, depending on what was available to the maskmaker. Masks can cover a small portion of the face or be much larger than life. Have students, working individually or in small groups, choose a type of mask they would like to research. Find out when, where, and why the mask was used, how it was made, and what it looked like. Then each group is to produce a life-sized mask. These could be simply drawn on oaktag, colored or painted and cut out, or they may be as elaborate and authentic as the real thing: shaped from paper maché, carefully painted and covered with shells, feathers, beads, buttons, fur, foil, curled paper strips, etc. Some suggestions are illustrated on the following page. Cover the bulletin board with black, royal blue, or purple paper or velvet. Cut letters to spell the words "Making Faces" from stiff paper or oaktag and use scissors and pencils to punch and cut three-dimensional textures in them before attaching them across the center of the bulletin board. Have each student or group present a mask and explain its appearance, use, and construction. Attach the masks side by side in rows across the top and beneath the title letters.

Chinese Opera
Masks

_____

_____

_____

_____

Udo (Death) Mask
of Borneo

Bamana
Rite of Passage
Mask of Mali

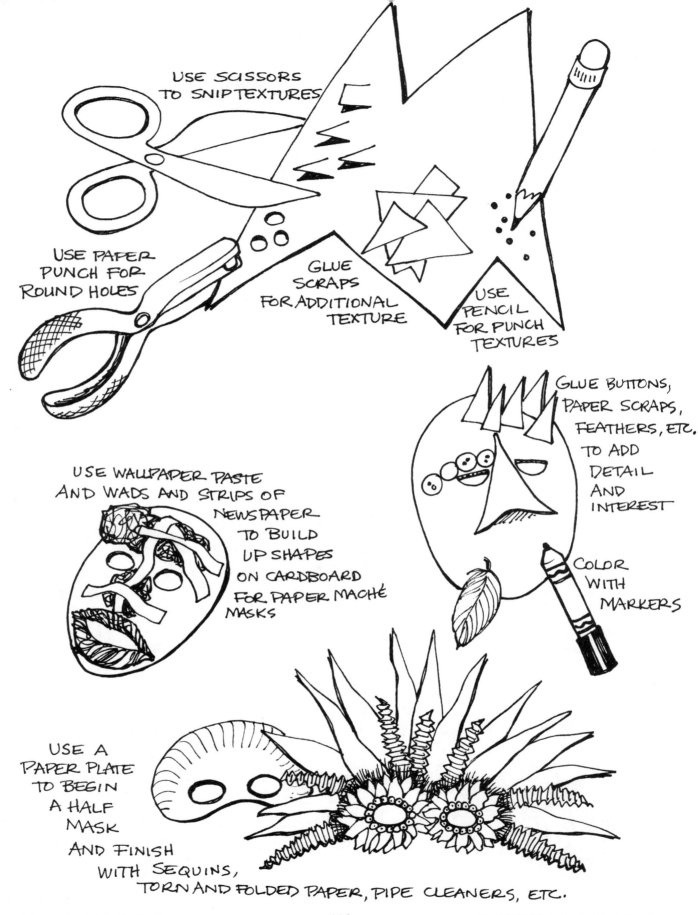

USE SCISSORS TO SNIP TEXTURES

USE PAPER PUNCH FOR ROUND HOLES

GLUE SCRAPS FOR ADDITIONAL TEXTURE

USE PENCIL FOR PUNCH TEXTURES

GLUE BUTTONS, PAPER SCRAPS, FEATHERS, ETC. TO ADD DETAIL AND INTEREST

USE WALLPAPER PASTE AND WADS AND STRIPS OF NEWSPAPER TO BUILD UP SHAPES ON CARDBOARD FOR PAPER MACHÉ MASKS

COLOR WITH MARKERS

USE A PAPER PLATE TO BEGIN A HALF MASK AND FINISH WITH SEQUINS, TORN AND FOLDED PAPER, PIPE CLEANERS, ETC.

ABCDEF
GHIJKLM
NOPQR
STUVW
XYZ abc
defgijhklm
nopqrstu
vwxyz!___...

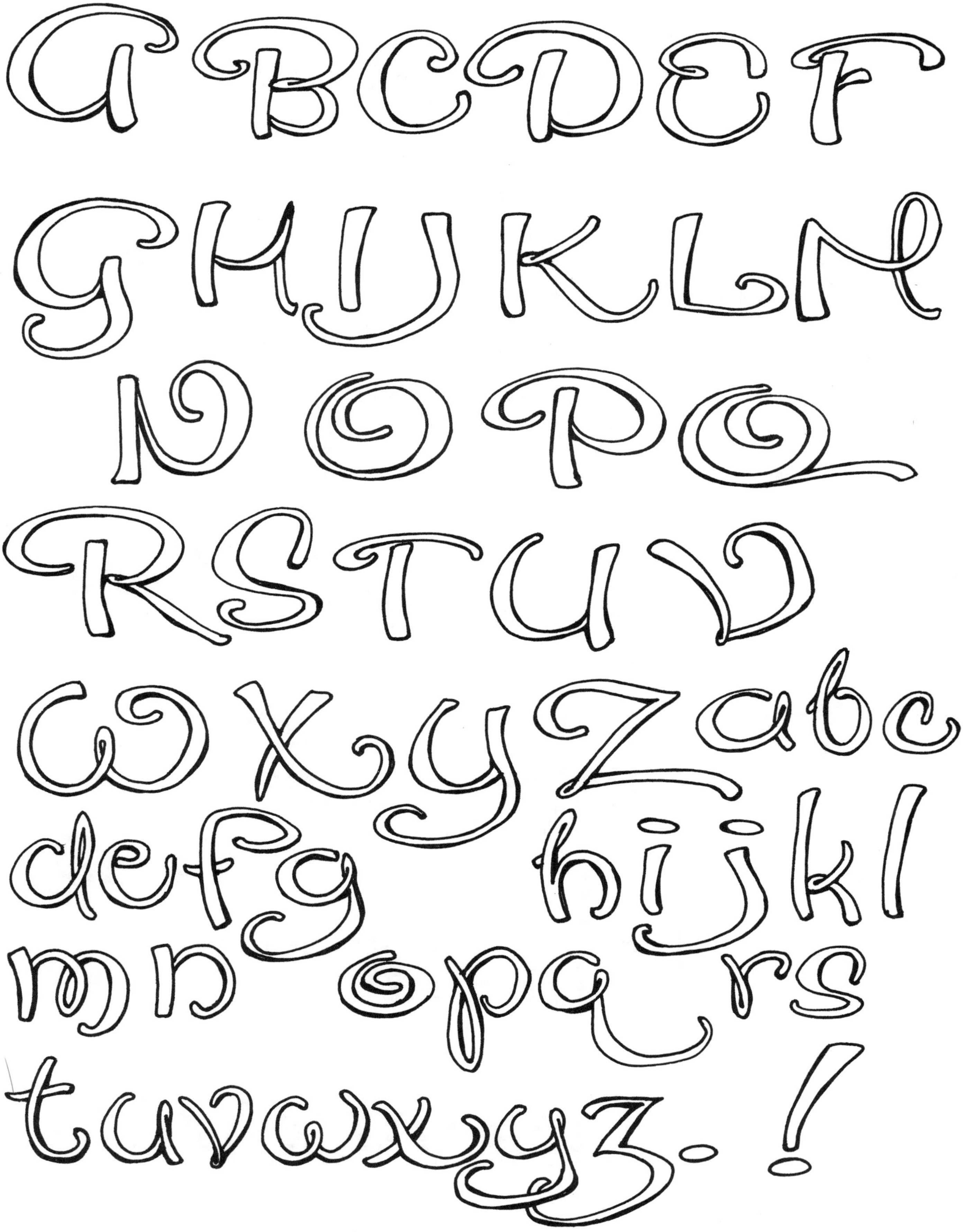

A B C D E F
G H I J K L M
N O P Q
R S T U V
W X Y Z a b c
d e f g h i j k l
m n o p q r s
t u v w x y z . !

ABCDEF
GHIJKLM
NOPQRS
TUVWXY
Zabcdefgh
ijklmnopq
rstuvwxyz